There & Then

Also by James Salter

There
& *Then*

The Travel Writing of

James Salter

COUNTERPOINT | BERKELEY

Library of Congress Cataloging-in-Publication Data
Salter, James.
There & then : the travel writing of James Salter.
p. cm.
ISBN: 978-1-61902-285-0
1. Salter, James—Travel. 2. Voyages and travels.
I. Title: There and then. II. Title.
G465.S243 2005   910.4—dc22   2005023928

Most of the chapters in *There & Then* were previously published, sometimes in a slightly different form. We thank the editors and publishers of these periodicals for their good work. "Nothing to Declare," *Le Nouvel Observateur,* December 2003; "Europe," *Esquire,* December 1990; "Cemeteries," *Antaeus;* "Paris," *European Travel & Life,* September/October 1985; "Siren Song," *European Travel & Life,* March 1989; "French Summer," *Esquire,* April 1989; "The Skiing Life," *Outside,* December 1992; "Classic Tyrol," *New York Times Magazine,* October 1983; "Europe's Longest Run," *New York Times Magazine,* October 1985; "Immortal Days," *Outside,* November 1981; "Victory or Death," *Esquire,* May 1985; "Roads Seldom Travelled," *European Travel & Life,* 1988; "Mishima's Choice," *Traveler,* March 1987; "Trier," *New York Times,* July 1985; "Walking the Downs," *European Travel & Life,* June 1988; "Paumanok," *Hamptons,* July 1986.

Excerpt from *Burning the Days* by James Salter, copyright © 1977 by James Salter. Used by permission of Random House, Inc.

Book design by Mark McGarry / Texas Type & Book Works

COUNTERPOINT
1919 Fifth Street
Berkeley, CA 94710

Printed in the United States of America
Distributed by Publishers Group West

10 9 8 7 6 5 4 3 2 1

To days that were

Contents

There & Then

Introduction

In early 1946, just after the Second World War, I sailed from San Francisco on a troop ship carrying hundreds of us and I remember arriving in Manila, moving slowly through the vast harbor where the masts and funnels of many sunken ships showed above the surface with the water around them brown, the rust streaming out like blood. The city was half in ruins but filled with life and there was still a strange, sickening smell in certain demolished fortifications that were like caves where the Japanese defenders had died.

I was sent to a troop carrier squadron. We flew to Okinawa where the only building left standing in Naha, the capital, was the post office. We flew to Tokyo, which had the odor of burned wood and primitive sanitation. It, too, was devastated.

Then I was transferred to another squadron, in Hawaii. For the next two years there were flights across the Pacific—long, seemingly motionless flights, the planes were that slow. I had a silver cigarette case engraved with the names of the places I had been: Melbourne, Sydney, Kwajelein, Guadalcanal, New Caledonia, Guam, and the rest. I found the list impressive although it was far from unique—everyone had been everywhere.

In Shanghai we stayed in one of Chiang Kai-Shek's own houses. The master bath, in addition to a bidet, had a barber's chair. A civil war between Nationalists and Communists was raging. Inflation was flooding China, every day the newspapers printed a new exchange rate for the yuan in U.S. dollars, a seven-digit figure that had jumped by fifty thousand overnight. In the hotel dining room the linen was white, and the waiters were serving fresh strawberries. Outside the square was dust, with a mass of rickshaws that seemed abandoned lying there. At any hour of the day or night, when you stood at the top of the hotel steps there would be movement, uncertain at first but then focused, and from among the men who had been sleeping beneath their rickshaws the one you had hired for a dollar a day and whose name you would never know would rise and trot forth between the long poles, ready to take you anywhere, even outside the city.

Whether all this gave me a taste for travel, I no longer know; I suppose a seed had been planted. For a long time, whatever the opportunity, if it meant travel I took it. I went to Europe for the first time a couple of years later. The doors to the world were opened.

To be in another country! To be under the spell of a name! Buenos Aires, Tahiti, Pago Pago! Perhaps not Pago Pago, which turned out to be a single street of sad shops and a combined police station and liquor store. We fly to an outlying island—quite small—a long way across open water. Finally it appears, shaped like a low, rounded mountain but with no place to land, it seems. At the last moment a landing strip emerges from the palms, less than a thousand feet long. With a thud and clatter we drop onto the ground. Beneath the trees people are waiting—outgoing passengers with cardboard boxes of possessions. Some of them are students returning to the States.

You go to places because you have heard of them. I went to Tangier after reading Paul Bowles. Of course, I didn't see that Tangier; I saw the unwholesome city—even the sand on the beach seemed filthy.

In an altogether different world is the train to Scotland, cutting through England at astonishing speed. Seagulls in the green fields. Men fishing in canals. A hundred miles an hour, the steel singing, the roadbed glass-smooth, footpaths flying past. Blue England in the winter dusk. Low walls of blackened stone. Light from our windows fleeing across trees, embankments, sudden house sides, then shadowy ploughed fields, calm as the sea. Lone lighted windows. Cars on an evening highway, drifting back. We glide into dark towns. In the mild, fading sky shines a single star.

A rich Italian woman I met said she always travelled with a group of the same people—friends. They were amusing, of course. What is the point otherwise? But travel often means being alone, pleasurably sometimes, sometimes not. If you can overcome the occasional angst, you may have the chance to see some interesting things, perhaps the same things the tour buses bring people to see, but purified by solitude, if you will. In any case, do not stay in the hotel room. That is the only place where you are vulnerable.

Beyond the rocks lies deep, milky sea. Surf is breaking on the reef. A girl naked to the waist is going in, a slender brown girl, the water making her nakedness gleam. The pagan life. The ancient dream of happiness. The palm trees provide fruit and shade. Life is stripped down. At the Sunday service the men are in lava lavas with white jackets and shirt and tie. The women in white dresses, some in high-heeled shoes. Their woven fans beat slowly as the choir bawls hymns. Through the window is the white line of breakers, and sun glinting on the dense green sea.

In Bordeaux the hotel was up a side street, the lobby filled with old magazines and the smell of cooking, but the room was large and well-enough furnished: a marble fireplace, mirrors, a desk and chairs, a bathroom like a pavilion. The bells of the church rang lightly on the quarter hours. At night there were fleas.

We drove to the Medoc. Beautiful vineyards, buildings bleached by the sun. At Margaux, in the alley of trees, the long green rows of vines spread in every direction, unshakable prosperity, rich for a thousand years. The estates are like nations, like great ships at sea.

Is it true? Is there a place that is Eden? An old hotel? The Rainmaker? Before the crowds came? Before money drowned us? The world earlier writers knew. Stevenson in the great house with wide verandas and the view of the sea. Pirandello in Sicily, where past the house and on a promontory he lies buried and you can see Africa, far off. Perhaps always in travel there is that idea of Jung's, of something already imprinted in us for which we are unconsciously searching. Sometimes not so unconsciously.

Nothing to Declare

Of course, I never expected to be stopped. People were just passing through Customs. I had one bag and a declaration on which nothing was written under Items Acquired Abroad. The guard looked at the declaration.

"You were away how long?"

"Eight days."

He was reading it,

"France was the only country you visited?"

"Well, I came via England."

"You didn't write that down."

"I was only there a few hours," I said. "I caught the train."

"I see. And the purpose of the trip?"

"Just personal."

"And you made no purchases while you were there?"

"The daily newspaper," I said.

They don't like jokes, I knew that.

"Would you mind opening your bag?"

He waited while I unzipped it and then, without a word, began to go through it, running his fingers along the edges and beneath the clothes.

"What's this?" he said.

It was an envelope.

"Nothing," I said. "Writing."

"All this?"

"Open it, if you like."

"You writing a book?"

"Not at the moment," I said. "They're just various notes."

"What sort of notes?"

"This is ridiculous. Personal memories, that's all."

"I'm curious. Give me an example."

"Oh, I don't know. Some nights at the Hôtel Quai d'Orsay, for instance."

I could have told him what immense value they had had at the time and how, years later, they still stayed with me. I could have said that if what was in the envelope was spilled out, there would be a fortune at our feet. The Hôtel Quay d'Orsay doesn't exist anymore like some others, in Paris, Bordeaux, all over. There was a little hotel in Montbard across from the station. It was owned by a chef who had worked on the *Normandie*. In the middle of the night you heard an occasional great express rocketing by. I had memories of Nice and Beaune and the house on the Ile St. Louis where James Jones lived for eight or ten years, of the Train Bleu that you boarded late in the evening, had dinner, went to bed, and in the morning woke with the Mediterranean just outside.

There were memories, too, of books I read in France that didn't then exist elsewhere, Nabokov, Donleavy, Beckett, Pauline Réage, the roads to the south that Cyril Connolly described, the old Coupole when it was a hangout, the streets named for writers, the terrible chill of winter when you had very little money, the wonder of it all, the misery, the marvelous language in which so many things were entirely different, some of them dizzying, the girl from the Sporting in Monte Carlo I met one night, the Winged Victory majestic at the top of the stairs.

There was that and much, much more, the things that you carry in your heart and that have made you what you want to be. I had lived all over France, a month here and there, sometimes a year or more. I never dreamed of becoming French any more than I did of being a woman. France was unalteringly different, ancient, stylish, beautiful, strange. I never tired of it—I belonged to another country and always went home because I had been born there and English was my real language.

He had pushed the clothes back into my bag and made some mark I couldn't see on my declaration.

"OK," he said, waving me through.

There was never any question. I had nothing to declare.

Europe

In Paris that first time we went straight to the hotel, from the windows of which there was nothing to be seen but the bleakness of buildings about forty feet away across the street. It was a wintry afternoon. Later we drove up to Montmartre to change some money on the black market.

The transaction, with a revolving team of Arabs in overcoats and sweaters, took place in the rear of the bar. There were silences, disputes, and frequent exits to check with a higher-up who actually had the francs. The air was filled with uncertainty and confusion. Before it could be agreed to, they said, they had to take $100 in twenties off to an expert to make sure the bills were genuine. They left francs as security and finally came back satisfied that our money was real. A few minutes later, however, on what might have been a misunderstanding, it all fell through, and the $100 was given back. It felt like notebook paper. A brief examination showed it was not the original $100 but counterfeit. It was the same money, they insisted, and started to leave. We stood between them and the door. They were smaller but they carried a reputation. We were calling the police, we said. Call them, they said, but in the end we got our money back. We drove off without francs but feeling streetwise.

Some years later I managed to lose a car as the outcome of a similar affair. The prospective buyer, an amiable man who said he was of Russian descent—I remember his name, Guivi—during our conversation grew to have such a high regard for me, he said, that he wanted my opinion, as a separate matter, of a man who was seeking employment with him. We stood discreetly at the bar in a café and he pointed the applicant, who was sitting on the terrace, out to me. He didn't look particularly trustworthy, was my judgment. As it happened, I was right. The visit to the café, as anyone should have known, was not for me to size him up but for him to look at me. When I left the hotel that evening he was hidden across the street and ready to make use of my absence. At midnight, when I returned, the car, which had been parked near the entrance, was gone. I never saw it again. Idle over the years, the distrust I had learned the first time in Paris had weakened and died.

But none of this is how the curtain rises.

There were three of us, Farris, me, and the club officer from Wiesbaden whose car it was. We had started early in the morning and had driven on empty roads. This was Europe and my first visit. It was 1950; Europe was impoverished. The plaster was cracking, the drapes worn to thread. Only a year or two before, it had still been for sale for a carton of cigarettes. The desperation had been vast and the testimony there before one's eyes: ancient telephones, outclassed cars, drab clothes. It had not forgotten, however, how to afford pleasure and the way to do things.

Farris I knew well. We were classmates, company mates, and afterward stationed together for three years. In this scene he is in his glory, about twenty-seven years old, in Europe on his first tour and living comfortably in the Schwarzer Bock Hotel near houses that had been flattened.

Sometimes on the street or boarding an airplane you see someone who has died, not someone surrounded by a nimbus or in white but the person themselves or nearly, until you get a closer look. I have never seen Farris, however, or his like. Judging only by that, he was inimitable. There were things about him that seemed almost equine, black hair like a mane, easy stride, and dark, lustrous eyes, but you could not own him. He might obey—in fact, he was dutiful—but he would never be owned. I admired him and liked him as one loves a horse—be at your best or you may be thrown.

Driving through outlying neighborhoods, grey and unknown, I had a poor impression of Paris that not even the Champs-Elysées, wide as a carrier deck and with only occasional cars, was able to improve. Paris seemed a dark, somewhat dishonored city that had managed to survive the war. The monuments and stone facades were black, but it was grime, not the smoke of disaster, that had stained them. The French had collapsed in the first round and surrendered the capital intact, an act in accordance with one virtue, prudence, but ignoring another, fortitude.

I spoke some French, the residuum of school days. The discipline of studying things you do not want to learn has fallen out of favor, although my own education leaned toward it. We read episodes of *Wind, Sand, and Stars* with the index finger of illiterates. The notion of a person, place, or

thing being masculine or feminine seemed to have no purpose, and the possibility that one would ever use French,
unlikely. It was merely another hurdle, like learning to dance.
I don't know where we went that night or what we drank.
The real memory is of dawn and an image like Mahomet's
paradise, driving through the streets with six girls and the top
down, a couple of them sitting on it, or beside us, a couple on
our laps. It was like riding banked in flowers; Montmartre was
grainy in the early light in which everything, every deformity
and cheap enterprise, every dirty restaurant and shop, was
pure. There is the Paris of Catherine de' Médici, at the Tui-
leries, as Hugo wrote; of Henry II at the Hôtel de Ville, of
Louis XIV at the Invalides, Louis XVI at the Panthéon, and
Napoleon at the Place Vendôme. But there is also the Paris of
those who did not rule, the poets and dreamers, and it was
the Paris of Henry Miller we were driving in. I had not read
him but I anticipated him, besotted, crazed, at odds with
everything and the next moment embracing it, in worn-out
corduroy, tieless, as he was walking home through the
streets; or perhaps I *had* read him and was steeped in the joy
of having it confirmed, this Paris where you wake bruised
after tremendous nights, indelible nights, your pockets are
empty, the last bills crumpled on the floor, your memories
crumpled, too. We went upstairs with three girls apiece and
the club officer napped in the car.

Paris. Early morning. Its cool breath, astonishingly fresh.
Its elegance and ancient streets, its always staggering price.
The sound of early traffic. The sky, blemishless and wide.
Somewhere in the gallery of love, where the pictures stir one
beyond speaking, the light, the divinity, the absolute poise,

where in rumpled beds at morning, in hushed voices, life is presented, somewhere in here I see a frame of Farris, an utterly intimate glimpse, his naked arm fallen from the side of the bed like Marat's. Then, as at many other moments, he was like a god, or if not, with a grace God sometimes bestows, the gift to every stag and hare but not to many humans. Then it begins to quiver, this image and indistinct room, the happiness is unquenchable and worth anything, someone is whispering, someone is laughing, there are cars in the street, the sound of water running in the room. It was all a game, the one I had been seeking, of the grown-up world. An hour later the streets reclaimed us; the night was past.

Near the Gare Saint-Lazare one night, Babel, years before, had seen a tall, beautiful woman in a low-cut, faded evening dress, waiting for clients. She was just like Hélène Bezukhov, wasn't she? he said to his companion. She might easily have been cast as the elegant figure in *War and Peace*, though her price was the same as all the rest. That first night, Paris was like that: It reminded me of something finer. In 1950 it was not weary of us. We were still handsome and admired; they smiled and turned on the street. The rooms were chill but they had proportion, and there was more than a hint of another life, free of familiar inhibitions, a sacred life, this great museum and pleasure garden evolved for you alone.

*

The parts of Paris that were revealed to me first were the least welcoming: the Champs-Elysées, the Avenue de l'Opéra, the grimness of the first arrondissement, department stores, and stations. I had in my pocket, for a first guidebook, three or four filing cards that had been written on by a tall, avuncular man with seductive charm named Herschel Williams, who'd been a fellow student in Washington. In his youth he had escorted debutantes, written a hit play, and probably been to Europe as part of an education, though he certainly went later on. Unscrewing the top of the fountain pen one evening in Georgetown, the leisurely act of a more polished world, he wrote down places and names for me as in years to come I would do for others. Inheriting Paris. The cards he jotted on have vanished, but I still remember landmarks, like a seaman who has seen, briefly and just once, a secret map. Restaurants I could not afford to eat in. Streets of the moneyed class. The nightclub he liked that has long since closed—it had violinists in dinner jackets and a bar of generous dimensions where after eleven thirty girls who had failed to find a client for the evening would show up, girls like those on the train in Maupassant's story, of whom the old peasant woman says, "They are sluts who are off to that cursed place, Paris."

Also recommended was the Hôtel Vendôme. That time I passed it by, but the approach to it I later knew almost step by step. On the corner where Rue de Rivoli and Rue Castiglione meet, Sulka, an expensive men's shop. Past it, walking toward the *place*, the sidewalk that was a mosaic of small tiles, cracked and sagging. Then the English Pharmacy and farther on, still beneath the shadowy arcade, at the corner, the tobacconist. The shop, though changed, is there still, dark marble around the display windows, in which there were pipes, lighters, and small gifts, perhaps a few guidebooks. Within, however, to one side in a tall case, were books of the Olympia Press and the even more disreputable—with, as I remember, pastel instead of green covers—titles of the Obelisk Press and the Traveler's Companion.

Here, unhurried, one could browse for hours. Ordinary life drowned, went under. On the street outside, often cold and wet it seemed, were passersby in overcoats and expressions of care, but within the shop one leafed through pages in a kind of narcotic dream. I bought *Our Lady of the Flowers* here, *Tropic of Cancer* of course, *The Ginger Man*, as well as de Sade, Burroughs, and later, Nabokov. The publisher of these distinguished books, Maurice Girodias, eventually closed up and was forced into exile.

He deserves more than a hasty footnote. He seems to have had a doubtful reputation, close to writers in their poverty and youth, probably not honest in his dealings, and cast aside by them later. He may have had defects, but I was not able to see them on the one occasion I was at dinner with him years later. His bitterness was unintense. We talked about the irony of it all and he was able to smile. For practical purposes he was still virtually in exile, he said, living in the twentieth arrondissement past Père Lachaise, with Paris nearly out of sight.

In 1958 or so I came across Girodias's edition of Pauline Réage's famous apostasy, the first cool pages of which were like a forbidden door opening and the rest, as I read, unable to put it down, like the shimmering of a fever—not since reading Llewelyn Powys, paragraphs of whose *Love and Death* I could recite from memory at eighteen, had my legs given way like this—I am not sure it harmed me but it affected me deeply. Though I thought about it a good deal, I rarely spoke about it, and this preserved it for me until one night in the book-lined comfort of Ben Sonnenberg's apartment in New York a young woman, when the subject somehow came up, told how she and all her friends at camp one summer had read *The Story of O* and talked about it incessantly. I felt disappointed. If schoolgirls could stroll through it untainted there was nothing to safekeep.

There was the Paris of hotels; they made up a kind of geography, like the names of islands, each with its own aura and size. The Royal Monceau, where the plush exhaled an ancient fragrance and you reigned in reduced-rate opulence. The France et Choiseul with its barren courtyard and poorly furnished suites; the Calais tucked in behind the Ritz; the hotel where the girl threw Damon's clothes out the third-floor window when he said he wouldn't pay her; the Récamier squeezed into a corner; the Esmerelda, Badoit outside on the windowsill in the cold; the St. Regis with its dark, gleaming wood and luxury, the light from above; the Richepense just off the Place de la Madeleine one winter, incredible loneliness, Prunier down the street where it was too expensive to eat; the Quai d'Orsay, hotel of hotels, sentimentally speaking; the Trémoille.

There was L'Aiglon, narrow and cream-colored, on the boulevard Raspail, with the lizard shoes of the famed director Buñuel outside the next room. Misty winter mornings, the cemetery eternal beyond the window, the ivied walls. Simone de Beauvoir in white nurse's shoes and stockings, her beauty gone, walking to the boulevard from the café on the corner where she often met Sartre for breakfast.

On one of the first night tables, with a glass top, I think, and a simple gold necklace limp upon it, lies a mimeographed list of restaurants provided by the air attaché. There was Androuët, judged unique because the meal was made up entirely of cheeses, and another place where the menu had been inspired by Rabelais with daring caricatures, and the Lido ("sit at the bar"). The Mayol, it said, and we went there. It was dank and old with worn seats. Girls badly fed, stage bare, costumes that had lost their sheen, and one lovely pair of breasts as if, amid it all, France was showing what it could be capable of. I searched for them in the program. The photograph there was a pale reminder, like looking at a passport photo.

Later came the Coupole, the old Coupole, with its din and thousand faces of who knows what—arrogance, intellect, art. There one was exposed to the old disease, difficult to cure: discontent. A producer who later died of an overdose, Jean-Pierre Rassam was his name, maverick, charming, was always there and always alone. He was certain, he said, that one night he would meet the woman of his dreams there and he didn't want to be with anyone else at the time. It was a misconceived idea: You are always with someone else.

There were places, in the beginning, at the bottom, rooms on an inner court with burned-out lights, when the city was unscalable and there were endless long errands in the rain or cold, handed-down newspapers, and skipped meals. You were alone with little money and not much nerve and a name on a piece of paper—someone working for a steamship line or in the embassy, who was never in the office or who never returned a call. And there were never-envisioned places, grand rooms in the Plaza-Athenée where coins slipped unnoticed between the cushions and trays of food lay half-eaten. Rooms barely paused in and rooms of a lifetime, rooms looking out over half the world.

It was the elegance and order of Paris, aspects I was not capable of seeing at first, that appealed to me, venerable things and strikingly new ones, the life of the streets and life that survives upheaval and death. The old count who lived on Quai Voltaire in the same building with all his daughters and their husbands. There was an American woman who lived across the way and took pleasure in always greeting him. One day she said she was going home, flying to America. The old count seemed interested. *"L'Amérique,"* he asked politely, *"est-ce que c'est loin?"* Is it far away?

Slowly one rises to a view of it all, by rooms, apartments, salons. You pass from window to window and scene to scene. In the Hôtel du Quai Voltaire the river was very close and the long grey curtain of the Louvre on the other side. Something overcame me there; I lay in bed trembling; my arms and legs ached. My skin was so painful I could not be touched. I had the flu, I thought, but it was more than that, I merely could not recognize the symptoms: It was hepatitis. I lay in the hospital for weeks, at first in delirium and then through long days, sometimes reading an encyclopedia of diseases and waiting for the report on the latest analysis of my blood. The starched white of nurses is a beautiful thing and so is the daily paper. It had been winter when I was stricken—February—and shakily I emerged at last into the spring of 1962.

*

The glamour, bouquets like the one tossed by Gershwin, the dirges of Jean Rhys, the nightclub singers, the style. The city is defined by all the heartfelt tributes of its chroniclers and admirers; they have created something even more enduring than the bourgeois city of stone. The Paris of Atget. Of Brassaï—he was not French; he lived first, as a child, on the Rue Monge—photos of brothels on Rue Monsieur-le-Prince or Rue Grégoire-de-Tours; lights of bridges in the mist, not a sound, not even a cigarette dropped in the water, the river stone-still; old Matisse with a nude model, nipples cherry black; the luxurious squalor of the studios, Picasso's, Bonnard's; nights of Paris, naked women with buttocks thick as hams and everywhere a grandeur, the parade; the hares hanging in the butcher shops, the silk clothes in expensive windows, and withal a supplication: *Grant unto me*, one is saying, *Bestow upon me.* . . .

On the Rue des Belles Feuilles a car with 77 on its plates—from the rich suburbs to the south—is stopped in the middle of the street, trunk open. Traffic, horns blowing, backed up behind. Occasionally a man comes out of a building with a box to put in the trunk. Finally, not in any haste, a woman in a long fur coat comes out—the blocked cars are in a frenzy—says a last graceful something to someone, gets in, and drives off without a backward glance.

Paris women, their eloquence, their scorn and esprit. In the *épicerie* another, in jeans and a Levi's jacket, a turtleneck with a scarf wound insolently about, fine features, magnificent body—brilliant, uncirculated, as they say of certain coins—looking at you without curiosity or shame and then back to regarding the display window. A tall, fair-haired man in a leather jacket is with her. She hasn't bothered to get in line. She merely tosses back her hair, breathing self-esteem.

Or the blonde in the Closerie sitting in a booth opposite a man but close to him, smoking, making slight, continual nods of the head as he is speaking, and looking right at him knowingly, as if to say, "Yes, all right, of course," and even more frankly, "Yes. You can."

They are not temptations so much as consolations, like the consolation of the proverbial, of things worthy to exist.

It used to be that you could be prepared for this by taking the boat to Europe, sailing on the *France.* You stepped into the perfection of the first hours onboard, the excitement and sounds, corridors blue with fragrant cigarette smoke, the walls of the ship alive beneath one's hand.

I think of the story of Styron and James Jones, who were sailing with their families—it was on the return crossing of the maiden voyage of the *France,* in fact. The Joneses were living in Paris then; they had a house on the Ile Saint-Louis and were travelling with a nanny, their young daughter, and a big dog. The Styrons had children with them, too.

The two men, in their invincible thirties, were out all the preceding night. They had met a couple of girls at P. J. Clarke's and were buying them drinks. Warm feelings drifted back and forth. You guys, what are you doing afterward? the girls wanted to know. Sailing to France, they said, want to come?

The ship sailed at noon. Jones had gotten home at seven that morning; perhaps he'd forgotten some of the events of the night before but as they passed the Statue of Liberty they heard, confirming all fears, shouts of "Yoo-hoo!" and energetic waving from the lower deck. "Who's that?" Gloria Jones wanted to know.

The girls had stowed away. Styron and Jones had to sneak down to the purser and buy them tickets, not only for the crossing but, when Gloria found out, for an immediate return.

*

There is the knowledge of the senses that includes carnal happiness, and a greater knowledge that comes from intellect and reason. In the life we admire, one succeeds the other but does not dislodge it. Sin, as a saint explained, is a turning away from eternal things toward things merely temporal; but not all such turning is sin.

Sometimes over Paris but more often in provincial towns there rises a comforting sound, a sound of reassurance, the voice of the steeples and towers, the bells. They divide the day at noon, the dark at midnight, and the hours between. They are a steadying and a warning: All is not ended, all is not flesh. There was an age of faith, and its bones, whitened but hard, are still part of the corpus of Europe. Many times in villages you listen to those bells and feel their restraining hold on the trivial and profane. You can read Hugo's description of the church bells of Paris as if standing somewhere on high on a special day, the first solitary tinkle, almost unauthorized, passing from church to church like the presence of a huge orchestra or glances within a vast choir, and then almost all together, at once, the concert, the *tutti* of the bells, as he calls it, rising from every part of the city, swelling, soaring, *nothing richer, more dazzling, more triumphant than this furnace of music*. Against the storms of life, which the Europeans know as well as anyone, there is this gigantic keel.

Europe is not only a great world but also, for the voyager, a far smaller one populated by only a few of one's countrymen, sometimes in the form of mysterious exiles. The real inhabitants take up no space. Eventually you may come to know a few of them but usually in a superficial way. Their language is their own and with it a definition of life. Still, a part of one's never-completed image is found abroad, things that defy proof: the graveled courtyards of old hotels where the car is parked, an early waiter or two in the dining room; or the warm bath holding a solitary reader of the dampened *Trib*, the scores of football games played far away, obituaries in three lines, and in the bedroom, eyes being carefully outlined in black. Evening is falling in Paris and you sit on a green wooden bench on Avenue Franklin D. Roosevelt reading the first letter in a week, it's about the book. She has read it for the first time in its entirety, a stunning letter that flutters in the hand like a bird as you read it again and again, cars rushing homeward, *My darling, I must simply say....* Nothing is like that moment. Everything you had hoped for.

The letter has disappeared somewhere and France is disappearing, too, the France of romantic myth. It died with the painters, with Ford Madox Ford, Lartigue, the ruined franc. We thought we had inherited history but we were merely part of it, the many leaves.

The world in which Edens lay unspoiled, Majorca, the South of France, the world that included the two great wars, that world is gone—a new, more dangerous one has swum into the light. All of that seems evident walking along the quais. It's different, the streets are filled with hornets, the cars rush forward in a wave. The city lives in a frenzy, all the cities, the academies, government offices, banks, bars, and shops; the buses roar past.

Kant had four questions that he believed philosophy should answer: What can I know? What may I hope? What ought I to do? What is man? All of these Europe helps to clarify. It is the home of a veteran civilization. Its strengths are vertical, which is to say they are deep.

The thing it finally gave was education, not the lessons of school but something more elevated, a view of how to endure: how to have leisure, love, food, and conversation, how to look at nakedness, architecture, streets, all new and seeking to be thought of in a different way. In Europe the shadow of history falls upon you and, knowing none of it, you realize suddenly how small you are. To know nothing is to have done nothing. To remember only yourself is like worshipping a dust mote. Europe is on the order of an immense, an unfathomable class, beyond catalogue or description. The young students are exploring sex, the older ones dining, the faculty is being carried off to the morgue. You progress from row to row. The matriculation, as an English king once said of the navy, will teach you all you need to know.

*

My agent, Kenneth Littauer, white-haired by the time I met him, knew France well. He was the first literary person I'd known, a description that might cause him to frown, and he opened more than one door for me. He spoke French perfectly, at least inside the door of the St. Denis, a small restaurant in the East Fifties that he favored, and in Connecticut he had a piece of glass about the size of a theater program with a bullet hole in almost the exact center of it—it had been the windshield of his plane when he flew with the French in the First World War; the bullet had only grazed him. He had been an observation pilot. Decades later he was invited with some surviving aces to a screening of old footage. The film was disintegrating and the historians wanted to know who, in the random scenes of various fields and swiftly moving figures, was who and what was worth preserving. "Well, Colonel," his partner greeted him airily when he got back to the office, "how did it go?"

"All right, I guess," said Littauer. "It was nice to see the golden boys come alive for an hour or two," he added.

We often talked about meeting in Paris sometime and having dinner at the Grand Vefour, which was high on the list of things he did not disapprove of, but we never got around to it. Over the years, however, he had taught me how to read a menu and the virtues of St. Julien. When he was seventy-four I had lunch with him one last time. It was at the Century Club and I had a presentiment this was the finale. He'd been obliged to give up his business—he forgot things, had no strength, he fell three times in one week, his wife had written to me. I expected to meet a broken figure, but he seemed the same as ever, stooped, untrusting, teeth blackened by his pipe. We talked about France and other things. I was living there at the time, which he envied. I needed to ask certain questions, those I had neglected to remember the answer to over the years: his favorite daughter's name, her husband's, the title of the book he had sometimes recommended to me, details of his father.

When we finished lunch he insisted on seeing me to the door. We walked down the three flights and in the entrance said goodbye. He had been a major at twenty-four, in France. That was after going over to the American forces. They had wanted him to stay in afterward and become a regular, but he decided not to. "There was no one to talk to," he said. Long ago. They had lit bonfires for planes coming home after dark. How closely we seemed linked. Years later I'd flown from that very field.

In the street I jotted down a name so as not to forget it, *Disenchantment*, by C. E. Montague.

He died a few months later, on Bastille Day, as it happened. By then I was back in France. In the obituary I discovered something I had forgotten or never knew: He had the Distinguished Service Cross.

*

We were living, my wife, children, and I, in the South of France then, still in its mythic haze, the South of Somerset Maugham, the Murphys, Gertie Legendre at Cap d'Antibes water-skiing in her diamond necklace. We were above all that, at least literally, in what was almost a village, near Grasse. The road from the sea led up through the perfume factories, and the smell of flowers, intense and sour, stung the nostrils.

The house belonged to someone in Connecticut I had never met, and had been occupied the year before by Robert

Penn Warren and his wife. I wrote to ask if they recommended it and a letter came from her in reply. It described a paradise from the windows of which, foil-like and glinting, the sea could be distantly seen. You will have the greatest year of your life, it concluded, if you don't happen to freeze to death.

The house, of course, had no heat. The goat that came with the furnishings was warm enough, amply supplied with straw, and even gave birth early that spring, but in the worst of winter the sheets were so cold we could not turn over in bed: We lay like statues of saints, rigid arms crossed.

On the far side of Grasse, in the country, lived another writer, John Collier. We became friends. He was in his sixties then, prominent once in the pages of *The New Yorker*, a cork on the waves, smiling, cherubic, not old, still quite green in fact, virtually a youth, he suggested. He came to dinner with his wife one night; we could see our breath at the table. "Do you have a problem heating your house?" I asked him.

"Only paying for it," he said.

He had large teeth and blue eyes, an almost ambivalent smile. An old buck, someone described him, but merry. He had come through everything, marriages, leaving England, the blacklist, financial ruin, and somehow made it to shore near Grasse in a huge country house said to have been the property of Pauline Bonaparte. He readily admitted his mistakes, they came bobbing along behind. He had been offered *The Treasure of Sierra Madre* to write when he was working in Los Angeles but failed to see a film in it. He was luckier with *The African Queen*, and had profitable interest even though his script was not used.

This was winter and spring in the depths of France. Van Dongen died in Nice that year; they were tearing up the paving stones and building barricades in Paris, and we were warned to be ready to leave the country. In town, tall blond Madame D's husband went mad for reasons of his own and would do nothing except play the tambourine. She was obliged to run the business; his mother, the house.

*

Lunch at Chez Maître Paul near the Odéon. Paris day, a table by the window, handwritten menu, immortal blue sky. The sky of Greece, they are always saying; this one, I say. Coquilles Saint Jacques in butter and herb sauce, *foie de veau,* Arbois wine. The chef, who is probably the owner—I've never asked—is visible in the small kitchen in a white jacket and toque. Between orders he reads, with the calm of an historian, the racing page of the newspaper. I can't imagine him betting, not today, not at work; he's engaged in study. When he went to restaurants he did not know, Fernand Point, the great chef, sized them up by the appearance of the cook— was he well nourished?

I think back to repudiated years and a man I once saw in a dirty movie house near the Gare du Nord. The lights had come on after the first film. Silence. There were ten or twelve men sitting there in the theater, waiting. He was much older than the others. A wonderful head of white hair like that of a restaurant owner or horse trainer. He pulled out a newspaper and began to read it, turning the big pinkish pages leisurely. It was so quiet you could hear the sound of them turning. A man who ate solid dinners and had a dog; perhaps he was a widower, perhaps not. He had seen a presentation of three young bourgeoises and what befell them, an impure work less interesting than its title. When the lights went down again he folded his paper. You could see his fine, impressive head in the darkness. I thought then of a lot of people for no particular reason, people who would never be found here. I thought of Faulkner one year when he was trying to work as a scriptwriter, driving down Sunset Boulevard on the way to work, unshaven, with his bare feet on the pedals and bottles rolling around on the floor. I thought of the Polish doorman, very tall, who used to work at the entrance to my parents' apartment building in New York. He'd been a lawyer in Poland before he fled but it was impossible here; it was all different and he was too old. He didn't have much to do with the other doormen—they scornfully called him the Count. I thought of Monte Carlo and the woman at the table who had asked me for chips. Afterward we had drinks at the bar. She wanted to show me something in her room, the clippings of her before the war when she danced at the Sporting Club; I was able to pick her out in the chorus. The English were there then, she said, lords; she had gone with some of them.

You were constantly—perhaps that was it—meeting people without money, people who amounted to something. Sometimes the more they didn't have, the more they amounted to.

Rising above the rest and very much of her class was a woman in London. She was a countess though fallen from the heights. Tall, with beautiful hair, she had once been a model for Chanel. I knew her for a number of years.

She'd been at a party one night where there was a film director, "this Joe Lozey," as she pronounced it. "I hate him," she said, "he's a bastard. He was saying what a great film was *Death in Venice*. I told him it was a beautiful painting but boring. He got very angry. *'Just who are you?'* he said."

Yes, who? Only the real crop of Europe, she might have answered, the originals from families centuries old. She was already a barbiturate ruin, breasts thin and drooping, skin beginning to go. She ignored it. Her eyes were heavily made up, her mouth curved down. She had a low, commanding voice and liked to laugh. Her words were slurred but her eyes were still clear, the whites startling. She was deflowered at fourteen by her uncle, and later, even after marriage, was the mistress of writers. She was imperious but very fine. She was also, in a large way, indifferent. She knew quite well what the world was, and in a sense, coming from a great family, she was responsible, but she could not be expected to control fate or the crowd. She was a woman who had loved deeply, and for years brought flowers to the grave of the writer whose photographs were in her marital bedroom; "He was buried standing up," she said offhandedly. Her own hands trembled as she talked and lit one cigarette from another. She was outspoken, impatient, and her wake stretched a long way back. Being with her was sometimes annoying but somehow it gave one enormous courage, the courage, really, to die.

*

Crossing into Switzerland where Joyce is buried; somehow he seems misplaced. The mountains dusted with snow, tumbling meadows, dark firs. It's snowing now; the air is suddenly dense with it, snow falling on the iron railings, the roads.

Basel, the old hotel on the river. Trying to write *ein Klassiker*. Basel with its great collections where Picasso sold for sixty thousand francs and Chagall for twelve hundred in 1939, the storm almost overhead. The Drei Konige, four or five hundred years old; the sheets were like fresh bank notes. We woke to rain, a typical European day, the leaves sodden in the street. Later it cleared and we walked. In a small sort of grove there was a couple at a table. She was young, blond, and carefully writing something. He was older. As we passed I glanced at the notebook. It was the alphabet—he was teaching her to write!

In Genoa the hotel was near the station and the trans-European expresses with a sound like heavy, channeled liquid swept by. The plane from Milan was arriving at ten thirty in the morning. She got off it. We rode the funicular to the top of the city. I was shaking like an addict, waves of desire crushing me. We hardly knew one another but she touched me as one touches a nervous horse. Don't worry, it said. She smiled.

Days without name, without number. . . .

I had driven to Rome once, for a few days, and flown over it many times, but in memory the train is how I at last arrived. It was to be a visit of several months. I had the name of a hotel and of two or three people; all the rest was unknown. Going by train you seem to become poorer and poorer as you enter the country, shorn of everything, language, understanding—you are alone but at the same time a feeling of latent riches begins to form. In this dense and littered landscape there is a new life like a legendary spring to be tasted and to become part of the spirit and flesh. Sacred Italy, yearned for by peoples of the north, colossal, petty, part of all our blood.

The sky is different in Rome. The blue of Paris skies is intense and passionate; of Rome, tender and pacific. It is a city of matchless decrepitude: faded colors, fountains, trees on the rooftops, beautiful tough boys, trash. A city immune to the urgencies of the north, a venal city flourishing through ages of brutal experience—nothing so often betrayed can retain a shred of illusion. A southern city; there are palms on the Piazza di Spagna and the sun incandescent in the afternoon. Rome is beautiful in the daytime. At night it becomes a little sinister, filled with the unknowable.

The city was first shown me by a clever, uneasy woman, convent-bred and bearing the scars—she had slept on a straw mattress there in the same bed as her mother and grandmother before her. The world was not a toy nor life a game. The second time we met she tested me secretly with five crucial questions concealed in conversation, the answers to which would pass or fail me. She never told me what they had been. From her stories I came to see a city of cynicism— no friendship unshadowed or without its compensatory side. The people were filled with humanity and warmth but also keen self-interest. The state moves from crisis to crisis, navies founder, banks sink, armies perish, but life goes on.

I am turning the pages in a small, greenish notebook, half the size of a postcard, with a Spencerian *Notes* printed on the cover, bought probably in a dimly lit shop near Via Bocca di Leone in the summer of 1964. In it are the invariables: people, telephone numbers, restaurants, clubs, places to dance, piazzas, beaches, wines, and things more unique, like the location of the cardinal's doors through the keyhole of which the dome of St. Peter's could be seen floating above the edge of the garden, exceptional streets, and the names of two whores who worked at the bar of a large hotel—actually one was South African.

From these ample hints I can almost recreate the period, though much is missing, many dialogues, certain faces. I can clearly make out the stocky, bald figure of Zavattini in a baggy blue suit of the kind that has buttons on the fly. He's in his apartment off Via Nomentana. There are bookcases on almost every wall with large sliding glass doors, every one of them locked. Behind the glass are thousands of books, mostly art books, and everywhere are hundreds of tiny paintings, portraits mainly, in wooden or gilt frames. Zavattini was a theorist and a dominant writer in the Italian films so powerful in their desolation and influence just after the war. *Shoeshine, The Bicycle Thief, Umberto D.*—I compliment him with the greatest sincerity on the important films he has written. Unmoved, he would rather be complimented, he says, on the films he didn't make. "The cinema has failed," he says flatly. They envisioned a new, fresh, politically meaningful art after the war, new methods of distribution, new ideas. It never came. He is still trying to convince Ponti or de Laurentiis to allow him to make one particular film for $150,000. The answer is no.

The films never made; they are like someone's last, unheard words, lost notebooks. No light will project them, no one in the future will endlessly imitate their lines. In the invisible universe where everything we know has its opposite, these unmade films will be playing and the others will be only dreams, in which case, as might happen if we could rewrite history, the world would be better.

Sometimes you manage to see one that has escaped from the umbra and like a tragic ghost amazingly appears. In Lyon once, in an old hotel, on the television I saw, with a feeling that it was perhaps appearing on my set alone, Orson Welles as Falstaff. He was speaking English and the abbreviated Shakespeare was in subtitles. I thought of Zavattini's unmade films, de Sica's, Pontecorvo's, all of them, like love affairs they would have given up everything for.

*

The farther south you go the less scrupulous life becomes, and Rome seemed to flaunt its decadence. "Jeem, they are reach," I heard, "everyone is reach." Even youthful beauty was meant to spoil.

Women seemed drawn to Rome, perhaps because of its feminine colors and the famous avidity of the men. There were women in expensive clothes staying at the Hassler or Hôtel de Ville; women with their husbands and without; young women who were actresses from Portugal and Yugoslavia—who knows what became of them; pairs of women in restaurants reading the menu very carefully; women stripped of illusion but unable to say farewell; women who owned shops and went to Circeo in the summer; divorced women who once had a life in Trastevere; English girls who said not this week because they weren't quite right—the doctor said it was nothing; girls who looked filthy, even unbathed, sitting in skimpy dresses in the restaurants, with young white teeth; *principessas* born in Vienna, in the shadows of vast apartments; and aging fashion editors who seldom strayed far from the Hilton. Against them, the legions of men: the handsome scum; the men whose marriages had never been annulled (almost all marriages); men who would never marry; men of dubious occupation; men from the streets and bars, of *nulla,* nothing; men with good names and dark mouths; swarthy men from the south, polished and unalterable, like the Italian teacher's boyfriend who was a *marchese* and had been sleeping with his cousin since they were both twelve, having intercourse in a way that Havelock Ellis used to describe only in Latin—the girls all did it this way to preserve their virginity, the teacher explained.

Amid this disarray there were somber sights, the great prime minister's daughter who was an actress, walking unsteadily through the restaurant bumping into tables. She had narrow lips and an actress's always-available smile. She was living with a black man on the Via del Corso in an apartment with high ceilings, no furniture, and the smell of incense. The front doors were lined with steel and had well-machined locks.

The apartment belonged to a Mafia figure, the black man confided, a very important man. "You know all those statues around Rome that have no heads? Well, he has the heads." It would be very comfortable when it was fixed up, she said. She had long red hair and pale skin on which there clearly showed a bruise on her cheek and another on her arm. Churchill, her father, was still alive. She sat down on the lone sofa with a drink.

"You've really got one going there," the black man commented almost casually.

"No, I don't," she said.

"Oh, sure you do."

"Have I?" she said sweetly.

On a magazine cover on the floor was a photograph of her that revealed him in the background. She picked it up. "It's the best article we've ever had done," she said. "Really, the most sympathetic, the most truthful. It's awfully good." In the light her hair seemed thin and wrinkles surrounded her eyes.

They were going to open a club together in Tangier. He was a musician and painter. Africa was the place, he said. "You just set foot there and the earth, it goes right through you, like you start trembling." His hands, infused, vibrated upward. "Ain't that right, Mommy? Maybe I'll be prime minister someplace."

She didn't answer; she liked the idea of Africa herself, someplace where it was easy to get money, she said. It would be nice to have a summer crowd in some place that was amusing, then in the winter, Lobo—that was his name— could paint. It would probably be a mistake, she decided in an added foresight, for him to become known as a singer or club owner first and a painter second because then, you know, people never quite erase that first impression.

In the countryside, chestnuts, dark and lambent, lay half-buried in the gravel of the gardens. The great yellow leaves, point first, came spiraling down. Untainted and unaltered, life here: the vineyards beneath the big houses, a man with his dog working in a field, wood piled by the door. The serene terraces of land, their views of hills and groves unchanged since the twelfth or thirteenth century. In ancient churches the Piero della Francescas slowly fading, like the end of an act, from the dark walls.

The thing I failed for a long time to understand was the connection between the vineyards, the great houses, the cloisters of Europe, and the corruption, the darkness, the mere riches. They are and have been always dependent on one another, and without one another could not exist. Nature is ravishing, but the women are in the cities. There was one night in Rome, one morning really, about two o'clock, when a man walked into a café near the Piazza Navona with two women, one blond in a blue-and-green silk dress, the other girl even better looking. He was in evening clothes. They sat down; the waiters began to stir. He smiled and after a moment he uttered two words, but with his entire heart: *"Beautiful party."*

*

The Via Dei Coronari, in the old part of Rome, was where I lived during one of the two seasons—one a summer and one winter—that I was there. The apartment was an *attico*, three rooms and a terrace, reached by climbing six flights of worn marble stairs. It was July; the city was a furnace and the apartment was the topmost, the sun beating down on its roof. Often I lay on the tile floor writing. The nights were cooler and I had a car. From time to time I travelled—I recall it as a period when I had plenty of money. The car was a Fiat convertible, bought brand new. The price, I believe, was $1,600.

I remember Rome chiefly as the location of the people who afterward, for me, disappeared. We sat one night in the garden of a country restaurant just outside the city, six or seven of us, a girl who worked for *Life* in Milan and another who worked in publishing, but the star was a singer already well known in Italy though not elsewhere. It was a long, unhurried meal with much wine. The singer was young and a bit heavy. Her voice was husky and experienced. Cigarette smoke poured from her mouth together with a rich, unfrivolous laugh. Like Lotte Lenya she sang Kurt Weill–Bertolt Brecht songs, but poets had written lyrics for her and she had begun to appear in films.

It was all about love, or more properly, desires. The serene face of a famous Italian movie star, she said, with its marvelous mouth—that serenity was because of the way she made love, with two men at once. A woman like that was always easy to identify—the mysterious smile, the lowered eyes. And they always glanced back calmly over their shoulder. Always.

There was a directory of desires; people were known by them. Visconti and the two handsome boys he had taken into his house as servants after they had been in his *La Terra Trema,* he had dressed them in uniforms. Germi, who left his wife for a young actress and what he found her doing the night he returned unexpectedly. The brilliant editor and the gypsy girl who was ten. . . .

Later someone told me the singer's story. She had begun as an actress, a rather shy, sweet girl who was given the chance to sing in a revue. She had to sleep with the male star of the show, of course, and afterward the producer. They kept cutting her part. She went to bed with the star's brother because that might help her, and finally it had to be with the stage manager. He took her to some house, a large one, and upstairs into a room. It was dark. Take off your clothes, he told her. When she had done this, he said, "Put these on," and handed her a pair of very high-heeled shoes. Then he had her get on her hands and knees on the bed. Suddenly the lights came on. There were other men in the room, all the previous ones, the star, the producer, the electrician. It was to be a kind of party and they came toward her laughing. She abandoned hope.

Keats also gave up hope in Rome. He was about the same age, perhaps a year or two older. He died on the third floor of the pink house at the corner of Piazza di Spagna. The room is there exactly as it was when the triumvirate of which he was part blazed across disastrous times, and his remains lie in the Protestant cemetery with the paired epitaphs. The school-girls listlessly passing through the pink house are more interested in the pictures of Byron. He was better looking, they whisper behind their hands. Outside the house, the Spanish Steps are always crowded. The pilgrims are countless though Keats is not among the things that have made them come.

*

My grandfather went to Europe often. He was a toy importer and had a German shepherd and a cane. Though we lived in the same city I rarely saw him and then only through the eyes of a very young child. The cane, I heard long after, had been used to smuggle diamonds. My father went twice, after the First War and during the Second—I am taking the liberty of calling England part of Europe.

I was summoned by many things, among them a letter from a classmate, which reached me in the far Pacific. He had stood in front of me in formations at school, gangling, unin-spirable, tall as a crane; I had met him early on and some-thing had flashed between us. *Dear Hooknose,* the letter began, the customary opening of the three or four letters I received from him over a lifetime, and went on to describe life in Europe, where he had been sent, in the spring of that year, 1946. The letter was enticing.

*

Some things I have left out intentionally, others not, and oth-ers because they are written elsewhere.

I've left out Sicily; Haut de Cagnes; London in the evening and girls seen in Rolls-Royces, faces lit by the dash; the German dentist in Rome—the bombing of North Viet-nam had just begun—"Good, bomb them," he said as he picked up his instruments, "bomb them all." I've left out the place in Paris that for a long time was the essence of the city for me, oddly enough an American household, that of the Abbotts. He was a friend who had remarried, the kind of man who might be doing it again in his eighties, and his new wife, Sally, was young and like a sheaf of silver. Witty, taut, she was like a new child in school who'd come from some confi-dent but difficult elsewhere, someone who made friends and also enemies quickly and who cut a swath; Nate was her sec-ond husband, I think. He had been a dashing Air Force colonel and now was the European representative for a large company.

Their apartment, in the sixteenth, was majestic; the living room opened into a kind of dome. The sofas and chairs were comfortable, the doors everywhere eight feet high. Late one fall we came up to Paris, four or five of us, from Chaumont, and that evening had drinks with them in the apartment. The city was black and gleaming, wonderfully cold. Nate drew me aside at about nine-thirty or ten. "Why don't you take them to the Sexy?" he said—it was a favorite of the president of his company.

I forget how we got there; there were photographers outside. I went in first to have a look. It seemed a place of style. "How is it?" they wanted to know when I came out. "Great," I said and we entered. "He comes here all the time," I explained.

There were a number of good-looking women. I think a band was playing; there was a bar. "Give me three hundred francs each," I said to them knowledgeably, "and I'll pay all the bills." Women were already introducing themselves. I could see Weiss and Duvall, neither of them inexperienced, exchange a brief glance as if to say, here goes. The money was gone after the second round. It seemed unimportant. It was like the night before the *France* sailed; the happiness was overwhelming. It went on and on, and though portions of it remain bright, where it happened is unknown. I've looked for the street since; it is gone.

Cemeteries

Divine died in a garret overlooking the Montmartre cemetery, the gorgeous, threadbare Divine who hated to have anyone walking over her head. The room is now famous, ill-drawn curtains admitting a thin ray of light, a halo of dust in the air. The room that was filled "with the chiaroscuro of poetic mornings." The young gravedigger is at work below, his bottle of wine sitting on a vault.

This is in a Paris so legendary that we have lived there as long as we can remember. A Paris crowded with the scenes of Victor Hugo and Balzac, the cynicism of Maupassant, the outrage of Zola. Paris of the painters and exiles, people one imagines elsewhere, Gogol, Turgenev, Synge. The Paris of voyages, avenues of luxury and commerce that will never die. Sexual Paris, glamorous beyond compare, Jean Gabin as seen by the dazzled eyes of a homely Violette Leduc, Paris between the wars, Picasso's Paris. Proust's.

I lived one fall and winter above the cemetery of Montparnasse, covered with fog many mornings, and walked to work through a vast, cold forest of the dead. The paths were empty and I looked at everything as I passed, growing dizzy with the flood of unknown names, the history of lives I could never know but that came to me in seductive waves, like conversation in Sunday restaurants when couples and families gather for lunch. The strange letters of these names bewildered me, made me imagine, like music heard when drunk. I inhaled them, together with a faint, sour smell that I took to be the odor of decomposition, "the gift of life passed into flowers," in Valéry's words, and I carry it with me to this day.

*

Kazantzakis is dead. Babel. Cavafy. Trotsky is dead. Carl Jung. The summary of their lives appeared suddenly in the newspapers. The next day there were others. Nothing can make a hole in mankind.

Many lie in foreign lands. The *vaporetto* steams out on the lagoon past St. Michele towards which, on almost every morning, a funeral procession of gondolas moves, led by the black and gilded hearse. In the cemetery of Venice, beneath the cypresses, Diaghilev and Stravinsky are buried, and Ezra Pound, as well as Frederick Rolfe, known as Baron Corvo, who died in poverty and alone in the autumn of 1913.

James Joyce is in Zurich with a headstone written in German. There is a statue of him near the trees, seated, one leg crossed, a book in his hand. Spectacles on his poor, blind eyes. The zoo is nearby. He loved to listen to the lions roaring, his wife said.

*

Beneath the dome of the Invalides, which was built by Louis XIV to house disabled soldiers, is the tomb of Napoleon, red porphyry on a base of green granite. The body is contained in six coffins, directly beneath the dome. Marshals and kings surround him as well as twelve huge statues representing the major campaigns. Above the entrance are his famous words, "I wish my body to rest near the banks of the Seine, in the midst of the French people I loved so well."

There is an elaborate myth that he lies elsewhere, that his valet who greatly resembled him is in the Invalides, and the emperor's body, like Alexander the Great's and Hannibal's, lies distant and unacknowledged.

"The whole earth," said Pericles, "is the tomb of famous men..."

No less a journalist than Victor Hugo described the funeral. It took place on the 15th of December, 1840, nineteen years after Napoleon's death on St. Helena. Hugo's own funeral, which was to rival it in size and splendor, was forty-five years later. There are few nations where a writer could be given such honor, but then not every nation invented literature.

The day of the emperor's funeral was bitterly cold with bright sun and a slight haze in the sky, Hugo wrote. Enormous crowds waited, stamping their feet to stay warm. The observations are those of a born writer, poetic, exact. He could write on a pad concealed in his pocket; he often sat at dinners taking down the conversation this way.

It is half past twelve. The crowd waits. They have waited for nineteen years. The bands play music. The troops and horsemen pass by.

From time to time the cortege halts, begins to move again.... Attention is redoubled. Here is the black carriage with its frieze of silver...

Suddenly the cannons roar at the same instant at three different points on the horizon. This triple, simultaneous noise encloses the ear in a kind of triangle, formidable and superb. Far-off drums are rolling in the fields.

The hearse of the emperor appears.

The sun, veiled until this moment, reappears at the same time. The effect is prodigious.

One sees far away, in the sunlight and haze, at the bottom of the gray and reddish-brown trees of the Champs Elysées, through the tall white statues that look like ghosts, moving slowly a kind of mountain of gold...

Far from the Seine, on Boulevard Ménilmontant, lies the dense and mournful garden of Père Lachaise. It was for a long time a property of the Jesuits. Eventually it came into the possession of the city of Paris, in 1803.

One can take the Métro directly there, buy flowers just outside the walls and walk for hours among immortal names not only of France.

Colette is buried here beneath the chestnut trees. On the wide, black stone is written simply, *Ici repose Colette*. Proust is here without an inscription. Rossini. Molière and La Fontaine. Chopin.

There is a reality to being present at the grave, like the reality, almost the aura one feels before a great painting. It confirms itself and also, in some way, the viewer. The two are forever joined.

Balzac is in Père Lachaise. Sarah Bernhardt. And Oscar Wilde, who died of meningitis in the old Hôtel d'Alsace, on Rue des Beaux-Arts, and went almost unattended to the cemetery. He had said he would never outlive the century, the English people "would not stand it." His monument was sculpted by Jacob Epstein, a marvelous god of stone in bas relief, immensely large, with a thousand carved feathers in his pinions and the genitals struck off by vandals. In their place is a crude inscription.

*

In the ancient world, graveyards, for reasons of sanitation, were often established beyond the city walls. The advent of the Christian era changed this. The catacombs were used at first as both places of surreptitious worship and mass graves. Later, when the religion was practiced freely, the dead were buried in churches and churchyards and for centuries this practice continued. Beneath the stone floors of the churches and in the ground surrounding them there began to be more and more corpses, until the bodies were being buried one on top of the other up to within a few inches of the surface.

Even this was not enough. In many cases the level of the earth was raised to the lower windows of the church. The air inside was often so foul that it became a source of disease and death to those who came there.

To make room for more graves, the sextons secretly removed the bones and decomposing remains and dumped them elsewhere. It became so systematized that for their work the gravediggers received the coffin fittings and even the nails to be sold for scrap.

The great, more or less public cemeteries began to be established in the nineteenth century. Montmartre was opened in 1795. Not as rich in personages as Père Lachaise, which opened later, it nevertheless has Stendhal, Berlioz and the Goncourt brothers as well as Alphonsine Plessis, the heroine of *La Dame aux Camélias*. And Madame Récamier, the beauty of the age.

Campo Verano, then situated on the farther outskirts of Rome, opened in 1837, and in London, with its huge population and consequent intolerable numbers of dead, the churchyards were finally closed in 1855, with few exceptions.

The immense funerary tracts belong to the rise of world cities. They are the dark hives that match the glittering, bright ones. Almost too large to comprehend and too dense to explore, they are part of the new era. In Venice, for lack of space, the graves of ordinary citizens are only temporary. After a number of years the bones are dug up and moved.

*

One hinge of the twentieth century turned at a drab provincial town in France where the principal industry was sugared almonds. In February 1916 the battle that was the tragic poem of the First World War began there.

For more than a year the struggle surged backward and forward, not so much in terms of terrain as of destiny, creating as it did almost half a million dead and a marshal of France, enormously venerated and loved in his time: Pétain. The memorable scene in *Grand Illusion* when Marechal bursts onto the stage and stops the prisoners' show to cry, "We've recaptured Douaumont!" refers to a key fortification in the battle.

The town is Verdun. Though there are war museums and relics and even portions of fortifications restored, the cemetery is the true monument. It seems that whole divisions have been buried here in long rows that curve slowly away. One is struck by the number of crosses that bear no names. Above it all, dominating the horizon, is a stark, white structure, half shrine, half mortuary. It is the Ossuaire. In basement vaults are the piled-together bones, or rather fragments, of at least a hundred fifty thousand men who were never identified or buried.

These incredible numbers, the remorselessness of the great death factory that continued night and day, winter, spring, summer, fall, in which men, horses, even cannon vanished in the mud and that ended finally in mutinies that spread like fire over half the French army—this immensity seems a prelude to what was to follow in our own time in another form.

André Maginot was a sergeant at Verdun and is buried there. He became minister of war in the 1920s, and the concrete and steel bulwark along the German frontier, the Wall of France that was to protect her for generations, had his name. The enormous cost of the undertaking almost crippled the nation, but the misplaced trust was fatal. In 1940, the Maginot Line failed.

Verdun twice shattered France.

In Westminster Abbey is a single companion to some of these countless dead: "Buried among kings, unknown by name or rank, brought from France to lie among the most illustrious of the land."

To walk the stone floors of this cluttered church is to walk on the heads of rulers of English as well as those who were the glory of their time, Dickens, Darwin, Samuel Johnson,

Hardy, Clive of India, Sheridan, Goldsmith, Handel, O Rare
Ben Jonson, Tennyson, Newton, Browning, Henry Purcell.
These names are only a bouquet. The full flowering is more
large by far.

And here also lingers an echo of conquests, of days when
an empire was founded on bloody acts. An exotic roll of
places, Gaza, Gallipoli, Scimitar Hill, embroidered on flags
and cut in stone, along with phrases that conceal by their
augustness the vast debris of battles now passed from sight.
Allenby's inscription: "...To the glory of God and to the
memory of the dead of the British who fell...the main host
lie buried in the lands of our allies."

*

Epitaphs, like women, are false, the poet says.

Still, we adore them.

On the tomb of Eleanor of Aquitaine, at Fontevrault, it
says, "Here lies a great lady of little virtue."

Yeats, in green Sligo, composed his own, too well known
to include here.

Jonathan Swift also wrote his for himself. *Ubi saeva indigna-
tio ulterius cor lacerare niquit*—where savage indignation can lac-
erate his heart no more. He lies in eternal exile in Dublin,
beneath the floor of St. Patrick's of which he was dean. Beside
him is his possible mistress, Mrs. Hester Johnson, celebrated
as Stella in his writings, "...justly admired and respected by
all who knew her on account of her many eminent virtues as
well as for her great natural and acquired perfection." Her
stone is smaller than his.

Elaborate, even epistolary epitaphs are common to the period and often strangely moving. Here is Congreve's:

Dyed Janey 19th 1728. Aged 56. And was buried near this place. To whose most Valuable Memory this MONUMENT is Sett up by HENRIETTA Dutchess of MARLBOROUGH as a mark how dearly she remembers the happiness and HONOUR she enjoyed in the Sincere Friendship of so worthy and Honest a Man Whose Virtue Candour and Witt gained him the love and Esteem of the present Age and whose writings will be the Admiration of the Future.

There are places one never forgets, the prairie graveyards of the American West, illiterate and poor; the German cemetery at Anzio with its Gothic handwriting in the visitor's book: "To my comrade, fallen on the road to Rome," or "To my dead husand; good father, good soldier, good man." These have been inscribed by people who knew a different life than ours.

In Rome, where the soft air seems to float memories, there is a cemetery described by Shelley as the most beautiful he had ever seen, the Protestant Cemetery. His ashes are there. In the days he saw it, it was almost a part of the Roman fields and even now it remains perfect and still, rich with curious inscriptions and sleeping cats.

Shelley was drowned while sailing in the Gulf of Spezia, and was cremated on the beach near Viareggio after burial in quicklime. Byron and Leigh Hunt were at the pyre, and Trelawny, now buried beside Shelley. In one of the unforgettable acts of a storied life, Trelawny seized the unconsumed heart from the flames. In fact, it was probably Shelley's liver, but the legend survives.

The Protestant Cemetery holds chiefly foreigners, non-Catholics, who died in Rome. Richard Henry Dana is there and one of Tolstoy's daughters, but it is in a section somewhat apart that another pair of graves form the most haunting union of all. On one stone is written,

> *This Grave*
> *Contains all that was mortal*
> *of a*
> *Young English poet*
> *who*
> *on his death Bed*
> *In the bitterness of his heart*
> *At the Malicious power of his enemies*
> *Desired*
> *These words to be engraven on his Tomb Stone*
> *"Here lies one*
> *Whose name was writ in water.*
> *Feb 24th 1821."*

And beside it in the corner grove, another; the blood falls out of your face.

> *To the Memory of Joseph Severn*
> *Devoted friend and death-bed*
> *Companion of John Keats whom he*
> *lived to see numbered among the*
> *immortal poets of England.*

Severn was a painter who in his old age became British Consul in Rome. He died in 1879. Keats was twenty-five when *he* died, his lungs eaten away, in a little room above Piazza di Spagna. He had been in Italy only a few months. Rome in those days had fewer than a hundred fifty thousand inhabitants.

There are epitaphs that are silent. At Wells, in England, in the singular cathedral begun in 1191, there is the tomb of Thomas Bekynton, the once Bishop of Bath and Wells. He lies in marble effigy, his stone cloaks are painted, he is as if asleep. Below this figure is a second one that horrifies. It is the putrefying corpse, tormented and rigid, agony written in every part, eyes gaping, mouth collapsed away.

Outside, through the open garden doorways of houses that are part of the close, there are tables laid for tea.

The dead bring us to life, vivify us, give us scale. We are the unjoined part of them and at their graves we stand at our own.

In Ruby Park Cemetery, in the once-famous silver lands of Colorado, the graves are unmarked. There is a single column of marble above a miner's daughter who died at the age of seventeen. The town of Irwin drew thousands of people in the 1870s, some from as far away as England and Scotland. The cemetery is abandoned. The mines have vanished. All but the silent warning,

> *My good people as you pass by,*
> *As you are now so once was I*
> *As I am now you soon must be*
> *Prepare yourselves to follow me.*

The dust of the pathway whitens our shoes.

Paris

I lived in Paris one winter in the 1960s in a wedge-shaped hotel that overlooked Montparnasse Cemetery, the Hôtel L'Aiglon. The rooms were small but comfortable. Luis Buñuel, then in his sixties, lived in a suite—I assumed it was a suite—adjoining, and his pointed alligator shoes were set outside the door late at night to be polished. Shoes were an important element in Buñuel's life and art and I regarded this pair with interest, especially since I never caught sight of the famous director himself or heard a sound from his rooms: no laughter, no glass breaking, not even voices.

This was the Paris, for me, of the Left Bank and its life, of James Jones and Irwin Shaw. The Joneses lived on the Ile St. Louis in a celebrated apartment always, it seemed, blazing with light. The Shaws lived at that time on the Rue de Grenelle. There was a restaurant not far away they often went to. One night it got very late—the drinking had gone on a long time and it was suddenly eleven o'clock. Shaw suggested going down to the local restaurant. It was too late, everyone said, it would be closed. In his rough, convivial

voice, Shaw said, no, come on, you'll see—we'll walk in and
faces will light up.

Le Dôme, La Coupole, Chez Benoît, those were the
places we went to. I knew Polanski, the editor of the *Paris
Tribune*, French actresses, writers, bar girls, dropouts. I knew
people who later became famous and others who did not—all
of them gone.

Years later, expecting to find an empty city, I went back to
Paris for a long visit. There were three of us. The first night I
opened the shutters of a room in a small hotel on the Place de
Mexico, and was nearly speechless. "Come, quick, look at
this!" I said. There at the end of the street, huge and lighted,
floating magnificently in the darkness like a space shuttle, was
the Eiffel Tower. I couldn't explain what I felt: everything, all
the memories, the days and nights. I nearly wept.

Paris can be many things—it is, after all, a great capital
city—but what truly sets it apart is what I felt again that
night. Visually it is overwhelming, not only the facades but
the beautiful color of its stone, its scale, the avenues, the
trees. To come into the city at night, flying along in the traffic on the Avenue de la Grande Armée, and to see there at the
end of it, borne upward by great slabs of light, the Arc de Tri-
omphe—that is an inspiring moment.

There are many stunning things in Paris life—the French,
as a friend of mine once remarked, have a lot of surface.
There are women, clothes, youths with beautiful hair speed-
ing by in Porsches, the handsome shop fronts, the many
things made with care and by hand—chocolates, bread, gardens, wine—the language, the deportment of the waiters, the
white tablecloths, the doors. There is a Paris of Balzac that

still exists, a Paris of Victor Hugo, of Turgenev, Babel, Zola, Proust, and Colette. There is a Paris of Hemingway, its resonances still strong, the light at the Closerie des Lilas, rooms at the American Hospital dedicated to women named Macomber.

You can visit Hugo's apartments, which have been turned into a museum on the Place des Vosges, and you can have lunch elbow to elbow with the stylish rich of the sixeenth arrondissement in one of their favorite hangouts, the Brasserie Stella—no reservations; everyone waits for a table. You can sleep in the room Oscar Wilde died in, in the now too perfect little hotel called airily L'Hôtel; you can dine in secluded bistros or stand near the spot where Louis XVI was executed by the mob. You are with the French, among the French, entering their buildings, seeing their art, eating their food, breathing their air, the air of Paris, which vivifies and makes one want to write, to think, to work.

You can see all this and do all this, but you can possess none of it, for in the deepest sense Paris is closed to the foreigner. That is the infuriating thing—you may touch and admire it, but it will never be yours. A woman who is Dutch but who lived and worked in Paris for years and speaks the language fluently told me a story. She was having tea one day with Madame Pisarro, the old widow of the painter, who complimented her on how well she spoke. The Dutchwoman was flattered.

"*Oui, vous parlez très bien,*" the old woman said, "*mais c'est pas Français.*"

It doesn't matter when you can cross Paris in a cab at the most ravishing hour of the evening, legs stretched out before you, splendid streets flowing past. You pull up in front of the bright terrace windows of La Coupole.

My old agent, Kenneth Littauer, who had flown with the French in the First World War, advised me when I was first going to Paris to stay at the France et Choiseuil, never mind about pronouncing it, he said. He suggested I eat lunch (and take the prix fixe) at the Grand Véfour but, oddly, he never mentioned La Coupole—it may have opened, in 1927, a little after his time. The food is all right, especially the seafood and grills, the service is good, but the ambiance is exceptional. The faces! You see *le tout Paris*, not only the Paris of today but of yesterday and tomorrow. You not only see them, you are smitten by them, you cannot imagine them, and they are always changing. I prefer the section on the right, over by the stairway—there used to be a second floor. You can sometimes be seated where you like in La Coupole, dine as late as two in the morning, step out and find a cab waiting in the middle of Boulevard Montparnasse, and drive home in the cool Paris night. It is 1930, 1960—the years never change.

I went back to the other old favorite, Chez Benoît. It was Art Buchwald, then almost unknown, who told a friend of mine about it, and he in turn took me. It had no Michelin star then. It was an old bistro on a disreputable street, Rue Saint-Martin, down near the Seine and Notre-Dame, but the house Beaujolais was excellent and the clientele solid.

It once was a classic Lyonnais place on a corner in the middle of the vice district, but the street has been cleaned up and has become a pedestrian mall. The food is as good as ever and the patrons even more well-heeled, but it seemed a little too bright and rehearsed for me this time. Was it really

better when I was having *boeuf à la mode* for the first time, I
wondered, when Paris was new? Or was it just one of those
things that have changed?

The *pneumatiques*, the little blue messages that used to be
delivered anywhere in the city within a couple of hours, are
no more; the rusty *pissoirs* that stood on so many corners,
gone, too. So is the Obelisk Press, which published pornography and also Beckett, Nabokov, and Henry Miller—a
forbidden green-covered copy of *Tropic of Cancer* was once the
trophy of a trip to Paris and threw open the windows for a
generation. The student hotels on the Left Bank that Cyril
Connolly wrote memorably of have all been refurbished, and
you can rarely get in them anyway—the Saint-Simon, the
d'Angleterre, the Hôtel les Marronniers—Paris is usually
booked. Les Halles is gone and with it the only "H" I knew in
French that was not elided. The painters and writers are
gone. Feminism has come to France, tall buildings made of
metal and glass sprouting here and there in Paris like weeds,
Mercedes dealers, fast-food chains, jogging clothes—all the
advances of recent decades.

"Paris is disappearing," a Frenchman lamented. "The language is being degraded because it isn't spoken properly anymore, children don't know anything about their heritage, the
history of the city—when they're running things they'll tear
it all down. It's very sad... France imports the very worst of
America. What's always been great about France, its real
riches, the French don't know anymore. All they know is the
wealth of money."

Yet one evening, coming in from Neuilly just after dark, I
passed the Maison Taittinger with its neon sign up near the

roof and the elegance of that French word, *champagne*. I don't often drink champagne, but I remembered fifty cases of Taittinger Blanc de Blanc piled up and stenciled with the name and New York address of one of the Rockefellers, waiting to be loaded onto the QE2 one November, and moving slowly along in the traffic of Neuilly, I thought of privileged French life, the life as it is lived nowhere else on earth, the black dinner dresses, spacious rooms, windows that look out on enclosed courtyards and gardens, the rivers, the automobiles, the love affairs. Along Avenue Foch, now somewhat *declassé,* the buildings are still not much higher than the enormous trees; there are whores on Rue Saint-Denis, birds in the bird market along the Seine, dogs on the subway trotting along beneath portraits of Ingres and Camus; you can park on the sidewalk and if you wake early enough in the morning see the men come around and open the pavement mains—the water pours out to bathe the city and they sweep the debris of yesterday into it with long straw brooms.

Paris disappearing? Not just yet.

Siren Song

Someone gave us the name of a Swedish woman who lived in Paris and owned an old house in a hilltop town in the southwest of France, somewhere between Toulouse and Bordeaux, not quite to the Pyrenees. It was in the *département* of Gers, which, it turned out, the French pronounce either with or without the "s" according to preference, a rare example of such indifference. Usually they will assume a look of utter incomprehension if even a diphthong is slightly mishandled.

It was winter and we were in France on a brief trip looking for a summer place, so we went down. The house was beautiful, situated above a large, walled garden just outside the ancient ramparts. The difficulty was the interior. Everything within, the arrangement of the rooms, the colors, furniture was impossible. The town, however, even in mid-February had a certain appeal. One long curving street of shops with a cathedral at one end and an old château far down at the other, quiet side streets, and in every direction countryside and well-tended fields. There was a hotel, several restaurants, and if things got too dull the larger towns, Auch to the south and Agen to the north, were not far off.

That was about as much as we found out. Through the tourist office, the Syndicat d'Initiative, which is a feature of nearly every French municipality, we found another house, close to perfect, a few kilometers from town and rented it on the spot. From the bedroom window, in the distance, the tower of the cathedral could be seen. It was an omen and there was something about the name of the town I liked: Lectoure.

The dignity of the name was fitting. Lectoure had once been capital of Gers. One of the oldest towns in the region, Gallo-Roman in origin, it had been a bishop's seat, principal residence of the Counts of Armagnac, and birthplace of one of Napoleon's most heroic generals. This was Marshal Lannes, the Lannes of Browning's poem, who enlisted as a private and rose like a meteor, illustrating Napoleon's famous pronouncement that every soldier carried a marshal's baton in his knapsack. Lannes was dead and a legend at forty. "I received a pygmy, I lost a giant," the emperor grieved. In the revolutionary reordering of things, the fine building that had been the bishop's residence in Lectoure was passed on to the marshal and later given by his widow to the town.

The château of the Counts of Armagnac also now belonged to the public as a hospital and home for the aged, and if you have to die in a hospital the one in Lectoure would not be a bad choice. Though only a local establishment, the height of the ceilings, the views, the large courtyard that has not been turned into parking space, the absence of gift shops and cafeterias not to mention the scale of it all more than make up for the lack of sophisticated technical equipment. Life was long enough anyway judging from the appearance of the veterans sunning themselves or making their way slowly with the help of canes and crutches up the street. Most of them smoked, too, which is further disconcerting. There is a dubious theory that the large amount of fat—butter, organ meats, *foie gras*—in the national diet together with the quantity of alcohol somehow counteracts the effect of cigarettes (and in France everyone smokes) but who really knows?

It is certainly not exercise that keeps the French healthy unless you count climbing stairs. The principal physical activity in Lectoure is trying to see the Pyrenees, which are about seventy-five miles away, and we had the thrill of nearly seeing them once, towards the end. Then there is *boule*, eternally being played close to the cathedral, beneath the trees. It would be difficult to try and describe this as a sport. The pace is about the same as in convalescence, and the strength it requires is the patience to watch it for long. Unquestionably someone will correct me and point out that *boule* really requires skill, psychology, tactics and, one might assume, unemployment.

The cathedral, which was built just before Columbus sailed to America, is without a spire that it lost, after a storm, two centuries ago. Despite this it is impressive, especially from afar. The same might be said of Lectoure. From a distance, particularly at night, it seems a considerable place, the floodlit cathedral, the boulevard lights spiraling down. As with other illusions, one should not come too close.

It's necessary, to complete the inventory, to mention the hotel, the Bastard—I never discovered the origin of the name. It isn't what one suspects since that is spelled differently in French. A distinguished eighteenth-century building with a graveled garden, almost in the shadow of the cathedral, it has elegant dining rooms but extremely small guest rooms, only some with what might be called a view, and a prominent local businessman, Patrick de Montal, who blends and ships Armagnac and other spirits including a superb liqueur called Fine Blanche, feels obliged to apologize to visitors when he puts them up there.

The hotel is owned by the town and there were furious arguments in the council over how it was to be renovated. Lectoure, certain members argued, though dependent on tourism, was never going to attract large crowds and therefore the hotel should have a limited number of rooms, ten or fifteen, for a select clientele. The majority of the council, however, were socialists and the word "select" drove them into a frenzy. They voted the idea down and also rejected the alternative of selling the hotel to a private party who, one suspects, would have probably seen that it should be something special. As a result, it is the chef and his wife who are the real assets of the place.

There's a movie house open on weekends, tennis courts down at the *stade*, a huge swimming pool overlooking the valley—part of the legacy of de Gaulle who had them built all over France to develop Olympic competitors—and a good though small archeological museum. Burying pipe or digging foundations in Lectoure frequently turns up ancient artifacts or coins and the area around the stadium, which was once the Roman burial grounds, produced important finds as recently as the 1960s. I asked Victoire, the wife of Patrick de Montal, about crime. There was none, she said.

"No robberies? Nothing?"

"No."

"They don't even steal cars?"

"If they do, it always turns out they're from Agen," she said.

Here, then, are some glimpses of Lectoure and the ravishing countryside around it during the summer.

*

There are some very beautiful houses in town. Good-looking people, too, one would assume, although they are not often seen on the street. Only once, when there was a wedding at the cathedral, what I took to be the upper crust of Lectoure was standing around Volvos and large polished Peugeots, well-dressed and with the pleasure and ease one often glimpses in France.

Meanwhile melons were being picked in the fields. Cars were parked just off the shoulder of the road and, further down, members of a family were bent over the rows. Wooden crates filled with melons were stacked at intervals. As I passed, the last member arrived. She was wearing white shorts, her legs were tan. A wire-haired fox terrier walked beside her. I tried to imagine the sullenness and complaints at her having to be out here instead of at the pool or with her friends but somehow it didn't go with her movements, which were natural and unconcerned—the rest of them were working down there, she was going too.

*

Figs, grapes, and quince were the original fruits of the region and in fact they are still combined to make something called *retiné,* the jelly of the poor. The quince trees are gnarled and distinctive. There's one in the far corner of the garden, which is appropriate since the Romans once planted them to mark the boundaries of private land.

*

Place du Bastion early in the morning, blue-suited men sweeping up leaves. On the road that goes down from here, just before a curve, there's a wide shoulder where they've put a bench and you can sit and enjoy the view, the area carefully maintained, like a park.

There are flowers everywhere, in every window and garden, on every curb and sill, the symbol of a people close to nature. Apart from their feelings about language, women, literature, wine, the land, marriage, and way of life, the thing I most admire in the French is their concern for the appearance of things—shop windows, *mairies,* avenues, parks, railway stations, houses; it has a soothing effect. You are in a country of symbolism, harmony, and order. The Romans planted the seeds for this civilization and, as they say of wine, the particular climate and soil did the rest.

*

They are French, like tadpoles are frogs, from birth. Outside the PTT a girl of about ten in a shirt and white shorts slides the motorcycle helmet off her head. She's just ridden up with her muscular young father. Her long hair falls down and she casually arranges it with one hand, the helmet in the other.

*

There is one secluded court, half-buried in the hillside, we always take. Nine in the morning, before the other players come and before the heat. The early clouds burn away, the sun beats down. The sound of the ball, the running, the fierce need to win. Monthly membership in the Tennis Club of Lectoure is $70 for a non-resident family, unlimited use of the courts.

*

Friday night at the Place du Bastion. The great trees have the strings of light between them. There are people walking dogs, sitting at tables or off on benches in the fragrant dark. A four-piece band led by an accordionist is playing music and children and couples are dancing on a wooden dance floor. There are women with baby carriages, boys playing *baby-foot*, young Romeos in dark glasses. At least twice as many people are watching *boule* as there are around the music. The *boule* area is brightly lit and there is only the faint thud of the steel balls in the dirt, otherwise intent silence. A girl is playing, the first I've ever seen play, a dark, flashing girl with a star tattooed on one sunburnt shoulder. It's like a working class wedding or the evening picnic of a particularly large—two hundred-odd—family. Beer on every table but no shouting, no women stalking off in tears, no fights.

*

The most beautiful of the roads is the one coming back to Lectoure from Condom. The first part, Condom to Castéra-Verduzan, is a single long tunnel through trees of luminous green, and from Castéra on, brilliantly rolling countryside of fields and woods.

Castéra-Verduzan is a somewhat mournful town strung along the road and has been a spa since Roman times. The waters are said to be good for diseases of the gums. In addition there's a good restaurant, noted for reasonable prices: Le Florida.

There was to be a performance of *Aida* in town, not the evening we were there but later in the week. The posters had a photograph of her naked to the waist, not unusual in France at this time of year, though we are far from the beach.

*

There's another good restaurant, the Table des Cordeliers, in Condom, in a converted Gothic chapel. There's also one in Terraube, a fortified village of the fourteenth century: Au Vieux Perron. From its windows above the valley, Lectoure is visible in the distance. *Magret*, breast of duck so thick and rich that it tastes like steak, is served everywhere in Gers. Here it is *magret cèpes*, with wonderful mushroom cover. There's a graveled garden, the restaurant owner is amiable, and the wine the local Madiran, Château d'Aydie '79, excellent, $9. The château of Terraube is in private hands but can be visited a couple of days a week and is the most handsome of those around.

*

The best restaurants are in Auch, which also has a remarkable cathedral and, despite only twenty-five thousand inhabitants, the feel of a genuine city. One of the nation's most admired chefs, Andre Daguin, presides over the Hôtel de France, a classic old building on the main square, and its restaurant. The hotel has twenty-nine comfortable rooms, many remarkable for their luxurious baths, and the standard of everything is like first class on an ocean liner.

Daguin is famous for championing the foods of the region, which means that duck, goose, *foie gras*, Armagnac, melon, and prunes are found in a wide variety of forms on the menu. He runs a two-star restaurant, one that in the lofty phrase of the Michelin is "worth a detour." The large dining room has a high ceiling, walls of a buttery beige, and orange and its shades abound. The napery is linen, the floor carpeted, there are fresh flowers on the table, and the dinner plates are edged in burnt orange and gold.

Daguin himself, in a white kitchen jacket, takes your order. In his fifties with the looks and authority of a film star, he is not given to frivolity and the meal is memorable with its final glory, *pruneaux à géométrie variable*, lying half-eaten on the dessert plate—there are no doggie bags in France, the dogs come to the restaurant and sometimes sit on a chair. The price of all this, wine and service included, a mere $115 for two.

At the far end of the room that night, Daguin, still in white jacket, was presiding over a long table of other restaurant people, among them his daughter who had come from the U.S. They were eating as jurors must eat, without a great deal of conversation. I kicked myself later for not having asked the waiter what dishes Daguin had ordered for the occasion.

A step, though not a very big one, down from the heights of the Hôtel de France is Claude Lafitte's restaurant on the centuries old rue Dessoles. Gers is Gascony, the native land of d'Artagnan and the Musketeers, and there is a Gascon temperament, robust, open, and courageous, which you recognize immediately in Lafitte. He is white haired, blue eyed, with a gleaming face full of life. The restaurant is in an ancient house, carefully restored and out of plumb. Worn tile floors, tilting staircase solid as stone, and also informality, elegance, ease. Here, too, the food is heroic. Huge slabs of toasted *pain de campagne* accompanied by local charcuterie. If not approached with caution, these will finish an appetite before the meal has really begun. Guest books are always suspect but the four leather-bound ones Lafitte brings to the table are an exception. There are pages of effusive and often witty inscriptions by people from all over, French, Italians, Germans, and someone who swoons over "the most beautiful cocking in Gascony."

*

As in all these towns the open market, held once a week, is an occasion. Farmers with their exceptional fruits and vegetables, the long, white vans of butchers and cheese merchants, the sides folded down. Vietnamese girls at a little table are selling spring rolls and small plastic boxes of cold fried rice. It takes half a morning to wander through and a week to eat everything you buy. Some things, like heavy round loaves of country bread, take a week and a half.

*

This is deep, domestic France, perhaps not unalterable but firm in its character and ways. Neither visitors nor money have changed it. That alone offers happiness.

The question they always ask is, how did you find this place? There was the Swedish woman to begin with, but there was something more. In this part of France you can still hire a man called a *chasseur de vipers* to catch any venomous snakes that might be on the property and remove them. If you ask how he finds them, the reply is he smells them.

That's how we found Lectoure. It was there somewhere and we trusted our noses.

The France of Kings

The Loire is the greatest river of France, and even if it were not, it still would be. Paris has the Seine; Bordeaux, the Garonne; Lyon has the Rhone and the biscuit-colored towns of the south, but the Loire, like the Nile, has scattered along it the most beautiful palaces and monuments of a country famous for them. As if the mansions of England, Venice, what is left of Newport and Fifth Avenue, the pavilions of the Bosphorus, the castles of Prague, all of it lavished on a single region that has remained relatively free of souvenir shops, franchise restaurants, huge parking lots, and other disfigurements. This is Touraine.

Naturally, it is not undiscovered. In the summer there are swarms of campers, many of them English and German, driving big sleeping trailers wobbling along the roads. Fortunately it's not necessary to visit in the summer. The spring is a good time to visit and the fall even better. You avoid the economizing crowds, and the only risk is rain.

The Loire, to begin with, is the longest river in France, some six hundred miles, and it flows a considerable distance northwards from its source near Lyon until making a crucial

bend to the west at Orléans, about eighty miles southwest of
Paris. Slowly, it then begins to reel off the great names: Blois,
Amboise, Tours, Saumur, Angers. Rabelais called it the garden of France, and there are endless orchards, meadows, and
vineyards along the river until it finally reaches the Atlantic
beyond Nantes. For a long time, until the last century when
the railroads took over, the Loire was a principal artery of
travel, and towns along it still have imposing stone ramps
leading down to the water. It is also still the traditional divid-
ing line between energetic northern France and the leisurely,
suspect south. A French woman I know who is married to a
member of an important family near Auch brought him north
to meet her parents during an early phase of their courtship.
"Not a bad fellow for below the Loire," was their judgment.

In the old days the aristocrats, ministers, and kings went
by coach as far as Orléans where the coaches were put on
barges for the rest of the journey downstream. Now you can
come from Paris by train in just over an hour or drive, which
is the best way, possibly via Chartres, only a slight detour
more than repaid by the chance to visit one of the greatest of
the Gothic cathedrals. The first view of it, rising above the
wheat fields as if it were built on air, is unforgettable. Then
gradually, as if willing to accept a lesser eminence, the cathedral seems to diminish in size as you approach and to assume
a more reasonable rank in the now visible town.

Chartres is important not only architecturally—its interior soared to heights never before dared and pointed the
way in the great age of cathedrals—but it also possesses
sculptural masterpieces and stained glass windows—173 in

all—that, apart from artistic glory, are the most important group of medieval glass still existing.

My one-time agent, an unrepentant man and one of the last to wear a three-piece suit in Hollywood, liked to travel in Europe and visit cathedrals alone, take a candle, as he said, and look at masterpieces. I think of him at Chartres, cleansing his soul.

*

One can see the Loire by bicycle—you can rent a decent bicycle at almost any railroad station along the Loire and drop it off at another if you like—or by train, on foot, or in that utmost modern invention, the tour bus, but the best way, in my opinion, is in a car, with a week or so at your disposal, and, tossed on the back seat along with maps and newspapers, three or four essential guidebooks.

The long, beautiful stretch between Orléans and Angers conveniently divides itself into two parts with the midpoint being Tours. Of the four châteaus that the green Michelin lists as being *vaut le voyage*, worth a special journey, two, Chambord and Chenonceau are in the first half and two, Azay-le-Rideau and Angers, are in the second half of the river.

There are nine more places including Amboise, Chinon, Blois, and Ussé, the château that is the well-known inspiration for the one in *Sleeping Beauty*, that are in the category of being "worth a detour," and forty-nine described as "interesting." It is true that in less than a day's drive you can easily go the whole way, but it would be like sitting on the Bateau

Mouche and thinking you had seen Paris. The Loire is worth as least four days, probably more.

You need a good place to stay. Fortunately there are many of these. Between Orléans and Tours are two towns to be recommended. The first, south of the river on one of its many quiet tributaries, is Montrichard where there is an ancient bridge and the ruins of a medieval castle. There are a couple of good hotels right on this tributary, the Cher, and in grander style is the Château de la Menaudière in its own park or the Château de Chissay—brochure in four languages—several miles down the road. It is claimed that Louis XI stopped at Chissay when on barefoot pilgrimages to Nanteuil.

Alexis Lichine liked the Domaine des Hauts de Loire a bit further away, in Onzain, on the other side of the Loire. It has every comfort and a good restaurant.

The two great attractions, Chambord and Chenonceau, are both within twenty-five miles of either Onzain or Montrichard, and Chaumont, right on the river, is almost within walking distance.

A huge, somber, fifteenth-century fortress with fine views and a disappointing interior almost devoid of furnishings, Chaumont belongs to the state and is indifferently run. Diane de Poitiers, the mistress of Henry II who had given her Chenonceau to live in, was its most famous occupant. In the fateful year of 1559, the king was killed in a tournament in Paris, struck in the eye by a lance, and his widow, Catherine de Medici, promptly moved her rival out of Chenonceau into this less appealing place where she did not linger long. Perhaps it was the furniture situation, then as now. Madame de Stael, exiled from Paris by her great enemy, Napoleon, also lived there. She had a restrained opinion of the views. They were admirable, she conceded, but she preferred looking at the gutter in the Rue de Bac.

Amboise, not far away, is also on the river. What is here, impressive as it is, is only a fragment of the huge structure that once existed, much having been torn down in the eighteenth century when no money was available for its upkeep. It is a particularly poignant place, the last stop in the long saga of Leonardo da Vinci. He was brought to Amboise by François I who had spent his youth here. These were the last years of da Vinci's life. He had paralysis in his arm that prevented him from working, but his presence was one of the stimuli that introduced the Italian Renaissance into France. The Mona Lisa was part of Leonardo's estate; the king bought it after his death.

A modest red-brick manor house called Clos-Luce near the main château was Leonardo's residence. Completely furnished, though with none of his paintings, it's worth visiting. The resting place of da Vinci's bones may or may not be in the small chapel of the château. His true tomb, in the words of the ancients, is the entire earth.

In 1560, a little over a decade after François I's death, there was another gruesome event that, when you know of it, gives Amboise a strange, melancholy air. During the religious wars, after an unsuccessful Protestant plot, the captured leaders were beheaded in the courtyard of the château before a large audience, and all their followers, some twelve hundred of them, were hanged. There were not enough gibbets for the job; Protestants were hanged everywhere in town—from trees, walls, and many from iron hooks set high up on the face of the château.

François I also built Chambord, immense and set in its own forest of more than thirteen thousand acres. The longest wall in France, some twenty miles of it, surrounds the grounds. A small river, the Cosson, was diverted to fill the moats. The king had wanted to divert the Loire itself, but was talked out of it. Lack of money was, as always, the factor that delayed construction, but neither wars nor the need for a staggering ransom for the king's two sons who were held by Spain stopped it. It took almost thirty years to build Chambord, and you will probably feel, as the courtiers of the time did, that it might well have taken less—the château is drafty and far too large, beyond all human need and on a scale that shrivels, rather than warms the soul. There are four hundred rooms, and when the entire court came with its servants, furniture, cooking utensils, and baggage, the great procession required twelve thousand horses.

The main feature of Chambord is a gigantic double staircase on which those going up and those going down, both figuratively and literally, could see but be separate from one another. Hunting was the chief sport, and François I, long-nosed and lusty, loved the chase. Around the roof with its hundreds of chimneys is a promenade from which the ladies of the court could watch such things. You can hire a horse and ride through some of the Chambord forest. There are stables two miles west of Saint-Dyé and also at the château itself. Twice a month, there are organized rides through parts of the forest normally closed off.

Molière wrote *Le Bourgeois Gentilhomme* at Chambord, and it was here that the composer Lully, in the cast of another of Molière's plays that the king, Louis XIV, seemed unamused by,

impulsively jumped from the stage and landed on a harpsi-
chord, smashing it to pieces. The next night the king expected
the jump again, but was disappointed.

After a fine dinner, perhaps at Le Grill du Passeur, which
is right on the river in Montrichard, followed by a memorable sleep, you are ready the next day for the diamond in the
crown, Chenonceau. As you drive toward it you catch
glimpses from afar through the trees. It seems to be drifting
in the meadows of a dream.

A marvelous conception, this long mansion, built on a
bridge across a deep, calm river, the Cher, is not only the
most beautiful but also the best run of the châteaus. I would
go to Chenonceau in preference to all the others, and return
to it first as well. It strikes the heart of something. You are
overwhelmed by the elegance, the serenity, the light that
floods the gallery on the upper floor. This one room spans
the entire river and you can stroll from window to window
and imagine it in autumn rains and the first sun of spring.
Chenonceau now belongs to the Meunier family, the chocolate manufacturers, but among its owners the most famous
was the woman who had it built.

Diane de Poitiers, the mistress of Henry II, was twenty
years older than he, although she remained remarkably
youthful looking until her death at the age of sixty-seven.
She was renowned for her avarice and her beautiful skin and
always wore only the black and white of mourning for her
dead husband, Louis de Brezé. Her influence over the king
was such that he took to wearing it as well. He turned the
proceeds of a national tax on church bells over to her to
finance the building of Chenonceau, prompting Rabelais's

famous quip that "the king has hung all the bells in the king-
dom round the neck of his mare."

There are fine gardens, and the interior has sixteenth-
century furnishings, tapestries, and painted ceilings. In cold
weather there are fires blazing in the huge Renaissance fireplaces. In this version of paradise, young women disguised as
mermaids once sang from the moats as the king approached
while others dressed as nymphs fled from the woods with
satyrs in pursuit. There were other brilliant occasions, including those attended by Henry III, when the most beautiful
women of the court appeared half-naked with their hair all
undone as might, in the words of one chronicler, befit a
bride. Henry III's well-known preference was for young men,
and the tableau may have been the idea of his mother who
was understandably concerned.

Chenonceau attracts large crowds, and although they are
well-handled it's better to go out of season. There are boats
that can be rented for a row along the river, drifting down
beneath the cool arches. Among the paintings is a portrait of
Diane de Poitiers by Primaticcio that manages to give an idea
of her character, and there is also one of the three Mailly-
Nesle sisters, two of them countesses and the other a
duchess, and each in turn Louis XIV's mistress. He took two
of them along on a campaign in Flanders, presumably to
avoid having to forage, but it caused an uproar, even in those
days of privilege, and they had to be sent home.

It's not a bad idea to have lunch at Chenonceau. There's a
small restaurant to one side, not notable, but a good place to
sit and read the guidebooks.

It's worth mentioning that one of the most beautiful roads

in the entire area is the north-south one from Onzain to Montrichard, D 114. A little way farther south, between Montrésor and Loches, is another extraordinary stretch that goes past the Chartreuse du Liget and other sublime, nameless buildings. Speaking of roads, N 152 along the north bank of the Loire is the preferred one to travel. Blois, with its chocolate factories and delicious smell, is where N 152 begins to run alongside the river. There are handsome old houses along the quai, walled gardens, flowers. The road is on top of a raised shoulder or dike, and in the villages houses are crowded against it with their ground floors below, on the level of the fields. The dike road is perfect for biking, level and with little traffic, legs of oak not required. Forty miles are travelled thus, Blois to Tours, past Chaumont and Amboise, both across the river like paintings. Then on past Ussé, Saumur, all the way to the end at Angers.

For this second half of the journey I would stay in the vicinity of Chinon near a village called Marçay or in the slightly larger village, Bréhémont, on the Loire itself. In Marçay is an exceptional hotel, the Château de Marçay, with a swimming pool and fine views. The clientele is mostly European, tanned Italians with sleek haircuts, couples, young families. Breakfast is served all over the hotel, in the bar, out of doors. It's like coming to a great country house. There are also excellent places to stay near Saumur, near Luynes, and in Les Rosiers-sur-Loire.

From both Marçay and Bréhémont, Azay-le-Rideau and Angers are an easy drive. Azay is a Renaissance masterpiece. Crossing the narrow bridge with its iron railings and driving into the main street of town, there are suggestions of something pale and majestic through the trees, something large but with a surprising grace. Azay was created at the same time as Chambord and Chenonceau, in the early years of the sixteenth century, and like the latter is built partly over a river. From the water side it seems to float on its own calm reflection. Balzac called it a diamond, a jewel. Its original owner was a financier who got into trouble, and the château was confiscated by François I. Largely though not completely furnished, it possesses the famous portrait of Gabrielle d'Estrées, the mistress of Henry IV, impressively formed and impudently naked to the waist.

The trip to Azay can also be made on a bicycle through rolling countryside. One summer, about halfway along the route, we came to a particularly disheartening hill and stopped to ask a girl in a courtyard, where she was looking after two children, if this was the right way to Azay-le-Rideau. *"Oui, monsieur,"* she said politely, *"si vous êtes fort."*

We occasionally saw other bicyclers that day. In the long stretch of woods, on a small sidepath, were two bicycles lying on their sides. Then we saw the couple, she lying face down in a patch of bright sunlight, pale naked back, white shorts. He sat nearby reading the map.

Not far from Azay is the town of Saché where Alexander Calder had a house and studio. A handsome Calder sculpture stands in the village square. A few hundred yards beyond, hidden behind massive walls, is the solid, bleached, sixteenth-century house that Balzac visited often between 1829 and 1835, set amid gravel walks with its steep slate roof high in the air. Across sloping lawns and beyond the hedge is the green forest wall. In the other direction, towards the village, the steeple of the church points to the sky.

The house belonged to a family named Margonne. Jean de Margonne had been a lover of Balzac's mother and was possibly the father of Balzac's younger brother. It was to this house, in retreat from the turmoil of Paris life, that Balzac came to write. He left Paris in the evening by coach and the next morning was in Beaugency for breakfast having had, one can assume, an imperfect sleep. It took the rest of the day to reach Tours where the Margonnes' carriage would meet him and drive him for two more hours to the house. The distance, in all, was 135 miles. It took twenty-three hours to make the trip and cost eighty-eight francs.

You can see the small upstairs room in which Balzac lived and worked from five in the morning until early evening, sustained only by countless cups of coffee and bread that he toasted in the fireplace. He would descend to join the family for supper, often reading his day's work aloud to them afterwards. As it happens, the house Balzac was born in, in Tours, and the one he died in, in Paris, are both now movie houses, so Saché is one of the most important sites still dedicated to him. In it you will also find the astonishing pages from his galleys in which he literally rewrote his books after they had been set in type. The margins and spaces between the lines are crowded with new words, sentences, and paragraphs. They are not only a fascinating glimpse into the task of genius but are works of art in themselves. Tours through the house are guided and conducted in French. They last well over an hour.

I visited the Loire for the first time almost thirty years ago, unaware of Fontevraud, the great, thousand-year-old abbey that was then serving as a prison as it had been since

Napoleonic times. It is now being slowly restored. Its plain, empty church is the burial place of four kings and queens: Richard the Lion-Hearted; his mother, Eleanor of Aquitaine with her unforgettable epitaph; Henry II; and the dust that was once the heart of Henry III. These royal figures are mingled in both history and fact, their remains having been dumped together in a heap on the floor during the Revolution and later reburied.

Visiting ancient buildings is like looking at masterpieces, apart from their beauty they offer a kind of exalted sadness. In the rush of modern times they give something else, a perspective. You gaze back on a millennium. Fontevraud belongs to a different world, a world now gone, of common faith and known status.

It was huge. The abbey originally contained separate monasteries for monks, nuns, lepers, the sick, and fallen women. Each had its own church, cloister, and living quarters. The most unique feature, however, was that a woman, an abbess, usually a woman of aristocratic, sometimes royal blood, was the head of everything. Fontevraud, in part because of this, was generously endowed and often served as a retreat, temporary or lifelong, for widowed or deposed queens and other persons of rank. Even at this point, the restoration gives a remarkably full impression of medieval life. There's a wonderful Romanesque kitchen, which is like a chapel or emperor's tomb, and the guides are particularly good. You'd also be wise to leave time to have a meal at Le Licorne, which has five or six tables and a Michelin star.

Past Saumur and the *caves* that produce and sell the white wine of the region is Cunault, an exceptional Romanesque church dating back to the eleventh century. Its town is a former river port, now asleep. You descend the steps of the church to the coolness and silence of a sacred world. There is the impression of, not whiteness but something more pure: clarity and light. The columns seem to run an incredible distance to the apse, and in fact the nave is slightly tapered, although the eye cannot detect it, to give an illusion of greater length. Except for sculpture high up at the top of the columns, for which it's worth bringing binoculars, not much ornament remains. The windows, without stained glass, are set high in the walls and there are faded frescos from five hundred years ago, Byzantine looking holinesses: Saint Germain, Sainte Emerace, Saint Christophe. Simplicity and lost grandeur, not easily forgotten.

At the end of the journey you come to Angers, with its wide boulevards and, brooding above them, one of the most imposing feudal fortresses of France. Angers is actually not on the Loire, but on the Maine, about five miles up on one of the few Loire tributaries that come in from the north. Nearby are the slate quarries that have roofed the entire region and half of France with beautiful blue-grey stone that has been quarried here since the twelfth century.

There are seventeen round, bulwark towers that, with the powerful wall connecting them, boldly characterize the château. These towers, about 130 to 170 feet high, were once even higher but have been partly pulled down. Along the highest walkways the German soldiers of the Second World War have scratched their names in the stone. The view is magnificent, as are the inner grounds, but the real treasure is a tremendous fourteenth-century tapestry illustrating the Apocalypse.

Originally 130 yards long and made up of ninety separate
panels, it is spellbinding in its imagery and vividness, more
reminiscent of, say, the Giotto frescos in Padua than the dark
colors and flat figures one usually sees in tapestry. The artist
was Hennequin de Bruges, and the work on it was done in
Paris between 1373 and 1380. During the Revolution it was
thrown out of the cathedral and lay in the street where it was
cut up for carpet, awnings, and even horse blankets. In 1843 a
search was begun to try and locate and buy back what could
be found, eventually some seventy pieces, now displayed in a
special hall. A couple of pieces have ended up in Glasgow.

There is also, in town, the Musée des Beaux-Arts, which
has a fine, gilded funerary mask of a thirteenth-century
abbess of Fontevraud and paintings by Chardin, Boucher,
David, and Ingres.

There are pearls scattered everywhere in the Loire, almost
too numerous to bother with unless you are returning for the
second or third time, the matchless Renaissance chapel at
Champigny-sur-Veude, for example—all that remains of a
huge château torn down on Richelieu's orders so it would not
rival his own nearby. Along the river there are rows of
poplars bending in the wind, the smell of hay and sometimes
tobacco growing in the countryside, sheep are grazing, the
great squares of sunflowers seem unreal. There are old houses
and walled gardens, the Château de Brissac in its elegant
park, still occupied by its owners but open to visitors in
spring, summer, and early fall. In Chinon, above the town in
the ruined château that dominates it, there is a large room, or
what was once a room, now open to the sky, where Joan of
Arc, simple, young, and illiterate came to present herself to

the uncrowned king, Charles VII, who, to make a fool of her, had someone else wear his clothes while he disguised himself as a courtier in the vast crowd. Joan was eighteen years old, a peasant, and she had travelled all the way from Lorraine accompanied by only six men at arms through the dangerous land. Advancing shyly, she disdained the false monarch and fell unerringly to her knees before the true one. The King of Heaven had sent word through her, she said, that the king would be anointed and crowned in the city of Reims. The world learned to believe her.

Five hundred years later outside the post office in town, a girl about ten years old, filthy, filled with life, her nails painted and a face like Rita Hayworth's, smiles and holds out a beautiful brown hand, the palm the pale of darker races. Ancient and modern days. The world of the Loire.

The river is slow and green. There are sandy beaches on the far side, shaded grass beneath the trees. Sometimes in summer the water is so low that farmers can walk their cows to graze on the islands in the middle.

You have a long, delicious lunch at Bréhémont on the wide path beside the hotel. You feel as Balzac might have felt at Saché—comfortable, secure, enhancing your girth. Silence, the leaves sleeping in the trees. The bottle of Touraine Sauvignon blanc is empty, the *mousse de foie de canard* a memory, the remains of a sautéed *épaule de veau* lie on the plate. The lunch was prix fixe, eighty francs. The sunlight filters down. What to think? Of things seen and yet to be seen. Of days lived and those to come. Some may be as good as this. The modest bill lies folded on a plate.

*

The first guidebook I placed my trust in, misplaced would be a better word, but which was the first of a long line, was Fielding's, a now vanished standard of the decades just after the war. It was to guidebooks what *People* magazine is to journalism and highlighted accommodations, that, especially in respect to plumbing, were up to American standards, then confidently thought to be the highest in the world. In those days rooms without bath in Europe were far more common and were to be, if possible, avoided. There were also important tips on shopping. There was something to be bought in every country, Borsalino hats, camel saddles that could be used as chairs, lace, brass trays, shirts, blouses, whatever—things that have long since disappeared into the garage or trash. The only tip of Fielding's that I remember gratefully was the Mediterraneo Hotel in Rome, clean and according to him conveniently located near the station, which as it turned out meant in a barren commercial district. One evening as I looked out the window I saw a woman moving about in a lighted room almost directly across the street. She would vanish for short periods into what must have been a bathroom, then reemerge, unhurried, unaware, and wearing less and less. It was dusk, the light was fading and the evocation was dazzling.

Still, this is not the sort of thing to be expected of a guidebook.

The indispensable for me is the red Michelin, published every year. Even if you have had your hotel booked by a travel agent and have little interest in food, it is still invaluable, an authentic dream book. Like chopsticks, it takes a little getting used to but is worth the trouble. It's an encyclopedia, a book you can get lost in, starting out intent on looking up one thing and straying endlessly, led onward by intriguing references or simple curiosity, planning vague future journeys or remembering past ones, as well as estimating the quality of hotels from their size, price of rooms, and location, which is often shown on precisely detailed maps that even indicate the direction of traffic on streets. These maps—there is nothing comparable—were of great use to allied intelligence during the war. I like hotels facing parks, cathedrals, in the old section of town or near the railroad station, and with the right sort of name. This last is harder to be precise about. Like the names of race horses, the champions always seem to have the right one. My inclination is towards the classic, names with France in them, or Royal, and a certain old-fashioned ring indicating, perhaps, rooms that are large, with comfortable bathrooms of a scale belonging to another era. In any case you can always drive by and have a look, provided you've been foresighted enough to plan your arrival for daylight hours. If it looks promising, go in and ask to see a room or two. In France they never bat an eye at this. If they do there's probably something wrong with the place.

In rating restaurants the Michelin has always been strict and unswerving. Its inspectors, dedicated in the way that postal employees and policemen used to be, provide, like the brass meter bar, one of the world's unchanging standards when they award stars. One star, it is said, will guarantee the restaurant owner a comfortable living, two will make him famous, and three, rich. My own preference has always been

for the one-star restaurants. I have eaten in twos and a number
of threes, but reputation seems to get in the way of them, and
they are usually places with an excess of forks and spoons.

Patricia Wells's *Food Lover's Guide to France* is excellent, if less
comprehensive, with history, anecdote, descriptions of
restaurants, prices, etc. Unfortunately its size is deceptive, it
weighs almost as much as a telephone book.

The green Michelin called *Châteaux of the Loire* is the other
essential volume. It covers everything, and there are essays
on the Loire as a region, its history, agriculture, the tradition
of the French court in the region, secular and ecclesiastic
architecture, stained glass, tapestry, wine, and more, all this
before the main part of the book that thoroughly describes
each château in alphabetical order. There is even recommended reading and a list of the châteaus that have *son et
lumière*—sound and light—performances. These can be anything up to two hours long and are usually well-done. They're
in French but even so, one gets the drift. All this in a slim
book not much bigger than many brochures or Hugh Johnson's *Pocket Encyclopedia of Wine*, which is also worth carrying
although Johnson writes very little about châteaus other than
those in Bordeaux, quite a different thing.

To round out the guides I would suggest one of the following: either *The Companion Guide to the Loire* by Richard
Wade, published by Prentice-Hall and perhaps difficult to
find but worth it since it is intensely interesting and reads
like a novel, or the *Dumont Guide to the Loire Valley*, very well-
illustrated and written. Simply because it's pleasant to read, I
would also recommend Alexis Lichine's *Guide to the Wines and*

Vineyards of France. It mentions hotels and restaurants, and Lichine is a man whose opinion you can trust; there are a few lines on architecture and many more on wines and vineyards. In a certain way Lichine's book is at the heart of France and reaches out to touch tenderly a great number of things.

French Summer

We were looking one year for a house in France somewhere in the country. Near a town that had a restaurant or two and perhaps a tennis court. The Côte d'Azur is all right if you like apartment houses, cars, and half-naked secretaries sunning themselves at noon on the beach at Nice, but despite its glories, it's a place that has been ruined by its appeal.

The search had ground to a halt. There were classified ads, mimeographed lists, and scribbled bits of paper spread on the desk, but you can no more tell what a house is like from a photograph and description than you can tell what a woman is like from her picture on the society page. We ended up going over ourselves in the middle of winter to look. At one point a French friend was calling on our behalf.

"The house is how?" she asked.

"What do you mean, how?" the unseen owner said.

"I mean, what is it like? Is it old or new?"

"Which are you looking for?" was the cautious reply.

"Old."

"Yes, it's old. It's ten years old."

"That's not old."

"Possibly eleven," the owner conceded.

I have always liked provincial France, the small towns. I like the way they look and the things that may have happened in them. You read Colette, an unforgettable fragment like *The Little Bouilloux Girl*, you read Flaubert or de Montherlant or see the films of Malle or Bresson and you are in a narrow world of passion, venality, and style.

When we finished the search we had four houses that seemed promising. They were in various parts of France, one down on the coast between Hyères and Saint-Tropez, one in the Dordogne, one a huge place up near the Loire, and the last in a town and *département* I had never heard of—Gers was the *département* and the old Gallo-Roman hilltop town there was called Lectoure. We couldn't decide between them, so in the end we simply took them all, each for a month or a little more. They ranged in price from $850 monthly to $2,500 for the big house near the Loire. We went over toward the end of April—it was spring but still cold—and came home when the pennant race was in its final weeks. The summer, already legend, had gone.

*

Between Saint-Tropez and Hyères the main road follows the coast. Just past le Rayol we turned off and went down toward the sea. There were trees and undergrowth on both sides, one or two houses, and just before crossing the right-of-way where a railroad once ran, the gateposts: Villa Santa Helena. The house was somewhere up on the hillside. The driveway gates were locked. Under a piece of broken pottery, as promised, the keys are found, but the one to the gates is missing. The baggage has to be carried up endless stone steps as the light fades. Also it turns out that nothing can be done to make the hot-water heater perform.

The next morning the *femme de ménage*, a Mme. Rignone, tells me that the gardener has the missing key. She's sure of it, but she doesn't know where he lives. "*Il est Arabe*," she explains.

A day or two later I heard the faint sound of a hoe down along the path. I went down to see. An old man in a golf cap, a skinny but worthy-looking old man with darkened skin, was at work. I introduced myself and he came forward to accept my handshake. What was his name, I asked?

"Ismael," he said. He had a cast in one eye and a two-day growth of beard.

He did not have the key to the gate, he said, perhaps the *femme de ménage* had it. I said I'd asked her and she thought *he* did.

"*Non, monsieur,*" he replied with dignity. The key, he said, was a subject on which he was completely uninformed.

I went back up to the house. Ismael. He had tipped his cap as I left and gone back to hoeing. Years ago he had been a child in North Africa. His mother and father were unquestionably dead, and he was working on a hillside in the south of France. He worked at other houses as well. It turned out that he had been in France for thirty-eight years. He knew the woman who had built the house and sold it to its present owners. A few times I saw him in town, usually with another man. They walked along the road slowly, like pensioners.

You know this house, of course. You've seen it in your

imagination, meandering, a bit bare, with black and white tiled floors, oddly arranged rooms, damp ceilings, glasses that don't match, and a hand-lettered sign in the W.C. that says ATTENTION and continues with precise instructions for use, disregard of which will result in your being *"les 1ᵉʳ victimes."*

There are terraces, books with water-curled covers, canvas chairs, and below on three sides the blue, immortal sea, the sea of Greece and Rome, of Ulysses, the bluest sea on earth.

It's a Bonnard house with a large bathroom like the one in which he painted his nude wife so many times. The tile floor, chilly in the morning, the simple kitchen, the living room with its many windows and doors, the small white car in the driveway, the unrushed hours—all pure Bonnard. He painted while the century roared past, the tremendous wars, crises, strikes, collapses, none of these are present in his work. There is no social content, only emotional, and it's that way with Villa Santa Helena, quiet, not a neighbor to be seen.

In the morning the light pours in. The sea is calm and smooth as a mirror, the sky a perfect blue. You can wake here with the woman of your dreams or alone or with two other families in the house and it is still beautiful. No one calls, no one stops by. The *Herald Tribune*, read in ten minutes, lies stuffed among the logs near the fireplace. Beyond the tall French doors the terrace is darkening, the first drops of rain appear on the glass. The sound of Chopin on the record player floats through the house. *Calme, luxe, volupté...*

Around in a far-flung semicircle are other towns, Saint-Tropez, Grimaud, Hyères, and beyond them, like a Vauban design, the salients: Toulon, Draguignan, Saint-Raphaël. They're comforting—something is out there. After a morning of work you can take a basket of lunch down to the beach and sit in the warm sunshine or go and see the yachts of rich men from the Bahamas in Saint-Tropez or the streets in the old quarter of Hyères, which was the first town in the south of France to attract winter visitors, well-to-do English.

The nights, which can be threatening in an isolated house in a foreign land, are the worry, nights without television or dinner guests, not even a good light to read by. Strangely, these tedious nights fail to materialize. Instead there is dinner on the veranda at eight thirty or even later, the sky still light, the tops of the sea pines waving gently beneath us, the rugged hills to the west beginning to be crowned by the intense silver light that precedes nightfall.

Stephanie, the blond au pair, is bored, her young blood lapping insistently. One Saturday night she goes off to Le Lavandou. Resorts out of season are melancholy—empty restaurants, closed shutters, not a companion male or female within miles. In the second place she goes into, though, she sits down, points to something on the menu, and the pianist, seeing she cannot speak French, comes over and finds out she's American. Well, he is, too. She meets an English girl and her French boyfriend and ends up at a disco, pulled out of line because she's good looking and let in free. Inside, the dance floor is so crowded that all you can do is bob up and down.

In the last part of May the small restaurant on the beach below town opens. The sea picks up a sparkle. Other people appear, Germans and English, white as paper. Summer is at the threshold at last.

*

At the end of the month we went to the Dordogne—rolling countryside, quiet villages, unspoiled rivers. The Dordogne is rural in the way France used to be—a rooster walking in the street by the *mairie*, beautiful houses along the river in Bouziers. Just to see this black, mysterious river from the cliff far above it at Dômme is something to be grateful for all one's life, Henry Miller wrote. He went even further. The Dordogne gave him hope for the future of the race, for the future of the earth itself.

Villeréal, the village we were close to, is not quite in the Dordogne; it misses by about five kilometers. It's actually in Lot-et-Garonne. The house was an old farmhouse on a property called Barbot, which means either a kind of fish (slightly misspelled), a man who lives off women, or a ladybug, no one knows which it's supposed to be. The town is a kilometer away, the only neighbor is Cici, a slim chestnut mare in a corral down by the river, the Dropt, which you can almost jump across.

The evening we arrived we went to find someplace to eat. It was barely eight thirty, but everything was closed. Bergerac, half an hour away, seemed the sole possibility, but in the first small town of the Dordogne, Issigeac, the lights of a hotel were on. *Oui, monsieur,* the woman inside said, of course we could eat. There were other people, a waiter in a white jacket, and the dining room had fresh tablecloths. We had a fine dinner and a bottle of *cuvée de l'hôtel,* which is usually a good thing to ask for. As we drove home I thought, Miller was right, there is hope.

In the morning I went into town to see if I could buy a newspaper. Villeréal is a *bastide,* one of an old group of fortified towns all built to the same general plan, with rectilinear streets and a central market square. It has a population of about thirteen hundred. I entered a place called the Maison de la Presse, which had a rack of French papers, and asked the man at the counter, whose name I later learned was M. Azaro, if he had any foreign papers. Would I like a Dutch paper, he asked? I said I was looking for something in English. *The Daily Express*, he offered? He could get me that. "Can you get the *Herald Tribune*?" I said.

"The what?"

It turned out he had never heard of the *Herald Tribune*, much less ever having seen a copy. I assured him it was a well-known paper, sold throughout Europe. He challenged me to find it on his distributor's list, which I did to his astonishment, saying that if he ordered it for me I would take it for a month. He said he would have it on Saturday, or Monday at the latest.

On Saturday I stopped in. An unfocused youth who, as it happened, was Azaro's son, was at the counter. Azaro came out from the back of the store. "It hasn't come," he told me. "It will be here Monday. Do you know where it's printed?"

I didn't, probably Paris, I told him, but other places too. "It goes all over the world."

"Is it printed in Geneva?" Azaro wanted to know.

"Maybe it's printed in Geneva also."

I had a foreboding as I went into the Maison de la Presse on Monday morning. At first Azaro pretended not to see me. I approached him. "Do you have it?" I asked.

"No. It hasn't come." There was a pause. "I believe they are having some difficulty printing it," he said.

I never did see the *Herald Tribune* while we were in Villeréal. It may be sold the world over, but it is not sold there. Later someone told me another story about Azaro, in whose shop, in addition to newspapers, one could buy stationery, fishing gear, and hunting equipment. It was some time after the Chernobyl accident, when fallout drifted over Europe. Bird season had started and customers were buying shotgun shells when someone reading the headlines commented that the paper warned it wasn't safe to eat game birds, because of possible radioactivity.

"No, no," Azaro assured them, "it's no problem. You just have to cook them a little longer, that's all."

I like houses with fireplaces, and the farmhouse had four of them, the one in the kitchen large enough for an old woman to sit in close to the embers, which in the past they did. On cool evenings a fire was blazing. The great shed along the side of the barn was stacked with wood. The smoke perfumed the broad, graveled courtyard. It was June and yet summer and fall at the same time—the bright skies of summer, the chill and rich smells of autumn.

The color is what one loves about this country, the sky, the fields, the biscuity houses and towns. The days are gloriously long. It would be dreary otherwise, since these houses, solid and comforting as they are, are not hives of light. When darkness comes, the French close their shutters, and not the slightest splinter of illumination comes forth. There is darkness in the churches, in the streets, the countryside. In winter it can be depressing, but one does not come to the Dordogne in the winter.

Françoise, the woman who rented us the house, was born in it, and her mother before her, and her grandmother before that. The family has owned the farm since 1812. They grow corn and hay, but there are also several acres of vineyards.

The mother, who is a widow, comes almost daily to the garden. She wears pants, a tweed jacket, and a jaunty fedora, bent over with her hands in the rich earth for hours. Yes, she was born here, she confirms, in the front room, which was her parents' room. Her daughter was born in the room in back. She asks me to bring an empty bottle and, unlocking the door of a kind of storage room with a dirt floor, gives me some of their own wine from a large wooden cask.

"Château Barbot," I say.

"Not exactly." She has a wise, honest face. "But it's not bad. *Ça passera.*"

In fact, the wine was one of our only disappointments. We finally had to pour it down the sink.

*

In midsummer we went north to the Loire, near Chinon, where the place we had rented, huge, dignified and pale, was called Grandmont, originally a twelfth-century abbey given by Henry II to the monks. It stands among walls, fields, and tumbled gates. For more than six hundred years it was in church hands and then was sold in 1790 to a family from Saumur. Later it was owned by a farmer who nearly ruined it.

Here, close to the Loire, the most beautiful of all the rivers in France, you are settled in the heart of history. Not half an hour to the east, near Sainte-Maure, is the chalk plateau on which in 732 Charles Martel turned back the overwhelming Arab wave that had swept across Spain and might have drowned all of Europe. Spain itself remained conquered for eight hundred years.

The stones of the house are that old, the deep window

embrasures with names from centuries past scratched in them, the thick oak beams in the ceiling hewn by hand. The scale and grandeur of the rooms, the timelessness of them, is pleasure. All around lies the forest of Sainte-Benôit. There are paths through it—one begins just across the road—but when you walk you must watch out for vipers, the *gardien*, M. Piffault, says. They're small, no bigger than a pencil, and a dark color. They also like the woodpile, don't reach in boldly for a piece of wood, he says. The *vipères* are poisonous, but there's one thing about them that's useful to know.

"What's that?"

"They do not," he says, *"surtout*, they do not like noise."

"Noise?"

"It disturbs them," he says. "When even the grazing sheep come in their direction, the vipers flee. The sound of mastication upsets them."

I accept this, though not as gospel. We never do see one of the snakes.

Chinon, down a single-lane back road, is about ten minutes away. It's on a river, the Vienne, said to be the cleanest in France. Chinon is the town of Rabelais, *petite ville, grand renom*, he said of it, and the most famous incident of the entire region took place there when Joan of Arc came to present herself to the king and in a crowded room, picked him out from among his gilded courtiers, as one of whom he was disguised. She had never seen him before, of course. In those days, it's astonishing to think, unless you lived in a town or city you might see only seventy or eighty people in your entire life.

In every direction are the great châteaus. To the west,

Angers and Saumur; to the north, Ussé and Langeais; to the south, Les Ormes, Le Rivau, as well as the town that Richelieu built and named for himself; and to the east the most ringing names of all, Chenonceaux, Azay-le-Rideau, Amboise, Chambord.

It is full, slumbrous July. We swim in the wide, flowing river or come well-laden from the open market, artichokes the size of melons, wine for fifteen francs a bottle, cheese of every description. Everyone seems friendly, even the dogs—there doesn't seem to be a pedigreed one in the entire town.

*

Finally we came south again, to Lectoure, and the ample, plain house of a Latin teacher in the local school. Beneath the huge chestnut tree in the garden, a lightbulb hanging from one of its branches, is a long, round-ended table made of white plastic. At this table in the shade, morning, afternoon, or evening, we sit. Dragonflies shift languidly along the ground. The wash is drying. The earth has an August haze.

What gives this house its quality are the views. In the distance, with nothing between but fields of sunflowers, meadows, and woods, Lectoure lies along the ridge of a hill like a marvelous abandoned wreck on a far shore. The seasons seem to pass before your eyes, autumn and its rains, winter, long-awaited spring. Through them the tower of the church with its faint trace of scaffolding stands against the sky. It looks almost Italian, the hospital at one end, the cathedral at the other. Between them is a long stretch of nondescript houses and walls that somehow gives the impression of a foreign coast. It's not a place the fashionable come to. Occasionally there is a glimpse of an insolent, stunning face driving slowly along the main street, but generally the level of excitement is a man I observed one day outside a café trying to teach a myna bird to sing the "Marseillaise." Still, it is a remarkable town. Along the edges it's like a fishing village, without the sea. That which stretches out beneath is vast and changeless. There are burnished mastodon teeth gleaming like ivory in the museum beneath the *mairie*, Roman coins, torsos from antiquity.

Near the end of the month there was a photograph in the newspaper of a nearly empty beach. A couple, the woman topless, were leaning back near their bicycles facing the last of the sun. In the background were a child and woman in a white dress near the water. On the blurred horizon, a lone white hull and sail. *Finit en beauté*, the headline said of the summer, ends in beauty.

*

This afternoon she came across the grass to where I was working at a small table in the shade. It had been four and a half months, and we had been everywhere, the sea at Arcachon, Paris, Bordeaux, Cap Ferrat, we had sat reading in the garden and walked across the fields to the ancient mill of a neighbor, ten minutes away, to buy bread baked over a wood fire, we had lived in cotton clothes, the backs of our hands were dark, there was one week left. "I love this life," she said simply.

I didn't answer. After a moment I nodded. That said it all.

Evening in Basel

You won't find the restaurant in the guidebooks, which is a pity. The owner—he was tall and wearing a sport jacket—greeted us at the door. Our table was waiting in the corner.

"And the food is quite good," she said as we sat.

The thing that finally makes a woman irresistible, of course, is what she says and what she does not. You may doubt this, but in the long run it is true. Looks, fine legs, these are things you can find in the street, but listening to an intelligent voice talking of things lived and seen—to feel the experience in it and, for want of a better word, the gallantry—there are not many things in life more seductive.

In America there is newness along with the idea that life can be invented, fashioned somehow from clothes, friends, television, and songs. One result of this is that things are constantly being discussed afresh as if they had just been discovered or were being initially defined. Europe is older. Its buildings, its languages, its ideas are all different. There is a distinction made between money and status. Flirtation is an art.

I had first met Bibi—this isn't her real name—when her

husband was alive. He was head of a large chemical company and came from one of the oldest families in a city where you are considered a newcomer if your family has been there for less than eight hundred years. She, though, was an outsider. She came from Vienna and had, together with sophistication, a warmth that made you immediately feel you were a friend.

Then her husband died—he was quite a bit older. She stayed on in their large house in a solid neighborhood near the river. There was a private courtyard and separate guest quarters. One of those women who seem beyond change, she was not beautiful but had a wide, knowing face, like Simone Signoret's. A well-travelled face on which there often appeared a smile. There was something immensely attractive about her, her well-made clothing, the expressiveness of her hands, the aura that surrounded her of companionship and ease. Certain things that in the past gave women their power have been thrown into the cauldron of equality, but she had not entirely abandoned the old ways. With her one felt that she knew what men were and what women were and had no difficulty accepting it.

At the house I had admired a small piece of sculpture. It was from a famous collection, which, it turned out, had been entirely sold at auction not long before.

"And you bought this?"

"No," she said. The collector had been a friend of hers. It was an interesting story, she continued. As a young man he had inherited a leather factory from his uncle. It was not what he wanted to do particularly, but he made a great success of it and began collecting art. He knew very little about it at first, but he made friends with the curator of the Deutsche Museum and every weekend they would travel to a different place and the curator would point out what was good and bad art and why. This was in the 1930s. Then Hitler came to power. "And he smelled something," she said, "He was uneasy, and he always knew things before other men did." Though he was a Jew, there was no problem getting out of Germany this early, so he had his entire collection packed and made ready to ship across the border to Switzerland. Goering, however, heard about it—he was a collector himself, and there was one painting, a Cranach, that he made known he felt should not be allowed to leave. Heller—let's call him that—didn't hesitate. He sent the painting to Goering and crossed the border with his collection without incident.

In Basel he continued his business and did even better than before. There was just one blemish in his life. As a young man he had fallen deeply in love with a girl from a rich family in Berlin, but his prospects at the time hadn't seemed good enough, and she turned him down in favor of a banker. He had never stopped being in love with her, and there was this great emptiness in him. Then the war came. She had separated from her husband and was living in New York. He heard this and managed to catch the very last boat to leave Europe. He had to share a cabin with three other people—he was used to having servants and every luxury, of course, but he didn't mind. He got up at three in the morning and showered when everyone was asleep. In New York he went to her and asked her again to marry him.

She agreed, but on one condition. The condition was that he arrange her divorce and bring it to her on a silver platter, without problem for her. Also one other thing: that

her children—there were two of them, a boy and a girl—
would be his heirs. He agreed. He went back to Switzerland,
and the divorce was finally arranged. It was no easy matter. "I
know that because I know the lawyer," Bibi said.

They were married after the war.

"She changed his house. She said, 'I don't like the salon; I
want a new floor, black and white.' She changed all the furnishings. She made him buy the neighboring house and tear
it down so she could have a bigger garden. She was a very
difficult woman. I met her at Bad Ragaz. She didn't like to go
to other people's houses, she never knew what she would find
there, she said. But she used to come to my house, it was
nearly the only one."

What their private life was like, Bibi didn't know. The
wife was up gardening until 3:00 AM and he, all his life, got
up at five. "Perhaps there was an hour or so between..." She
made a gesture of uncertainty and laughed.

When his wife died, Heller had no one, and he turned to
Bibi. She became his hostess. Three nights a week he gave
dinners and the fourth was just for them. He lived well, she
said, the best food, the most beautiful pictures. He always
had the guests leave by ten.

"He was a man," she explained, "whose advice on everything was good. If he told you, buy these shares, you bought
them and they went up. When he died, he didn't do what
was expected. He left instructions that his stepchildren were
not to be allowed in the house. Everything he had was sold at
auction. He didn't want his stepchildren to have his pictures;
if they wanted one they could buy it at auction. The money,
all that was realized, went to them, but not the marvelous
pictures."

She had had her own trouble with stepchildren, also two of them. When she met her husband he had already broken up with his wife, but the children didn't like her. She was straightforward with them. They were always welcome in her house, she told them. "Look, come," she said. "If we are friends, good. If we are not, then we are not." After their father died, they began to see her more and more until now they were very close to her. Even the ex-wife was friendly. Neither she nor the ex-wife had remarried.

"Marriage is too long anyway," I said. "Fifty or sixty years with the same person, it's too much."

"In any case," she said, "you have to arrange things. It has to be open. You do what interests you and let the other do what interests him. One thing, though—it's not good to tell about anyone else. If you have a little love affair, fine, but don't come back and say she had such lovely legs or hair. That's your own business. Here, would you like some of my *spaetli?*" she offered.

A little later she told me something I had not known that surprised me. She had been married before, in Vienna, when she was young.

"What did he do?" I asked.

"Not enough. I got tired," she said.

Cigarettes, bedroom furniture, evening clothes, money crumpled near the perfume bottles, grey buildings outside, somehow I saw it. She is twenty-two, bored, not a line in her expressive face. Then she said something else. She had had a child.

"I didn't know that."

"A little boy," she said.

"Where is he now?"

"He died. It was a brain tumor," she said simply. "He was only two."

Her face had no bitterness, no grief. It was the face of civilized Europe that had gone through unimaginable nightmares, devastation, air raid sirens, black headlines, political disaster, the face of Europe afterwards.

"He was absolutely normal," she went on, "and then...It began when he would fall down and hit his elbow, for instance. He would cry and hold his head, it hurt him there."

It was what happened and probably nothing could have kept from happening. She had had one bad husband and one good one. Now there was the house in Basel and another in the south of France where she went twice a year, in the spring and in the fall. She had sisters and a brother, nieces and a nephew—there was a lot.

People had left the restaurant. The owner sent over a liqueur.

"It's more difficult for a woman," she said. "A man can always, at fifty or sixty, start a new life, but a woman is used up. It isn't fair, but that's the way it is."

There was not the least self-pity in it. The great lesson to be learned from art, books, or people is still, how to live. Her face was quite composed. I liked looking at it. She had told me only a tiny portion of what she knew. I was thinking of another woman whose talents E. M. Forster had admired. A woman, he described, exquisite in her perceptions, tolerant in her judgments, advanced in her morality, vivid in her delineation of character, expert in her knowledge of three capitals...Scheherazade. A woman of that sort that was across from me.

We walked along together in darkness. I needn't go with her, she protested, she was perfectly all right by herself. It was, after all, Basel. It was late in the fall. The Rhine was black as a mirror with reflections of light on its surface. On the way back to the hotel I thought I could smell, though it was hundreds of miles to the north, the clean air of the open sea.

The Skiing Life

We left Munich in the morning and had lunch near Garmisch at a restaurant on the edge of a frozen pond. From there we drove on to Innsbruck and towards the Arlberg and St. Anton. By then it was late in the day.

How pure it all was, how carefree. The road had begun to be icy. It started to snow. Three or four miles from St. Anton a train went past us in the dusk with lighted windows, the swift, slender cars. In town the streets were snow covered and there were barns mixed in with the houses and hotels.

We were skiing for the first time, or almost the first—I had previously been for a day or two—moved by images of elegant-looking people and the names of certain towns. The instructors—farmers and carpenters—spoke English, since the British had been coming there for years. We went up with unfamiliar equipment in a cable car, a long, unsettling ride. It was just ten years after the war, and life in Europe was still hard. There were people who had walked up, unable to afford a ticket, starting before daylight and sitting in the sun at the top eating bread and cheese from their knapsacks before starting down. There were others with only one leg.

The snow was deep that first day. I was in the wrong class; I fell at every turn. The head instructor motioned me over after lunch. "I thought you could do stem turns," he said, since that was what I had told him. "I thought so, too," I said.

In the beginning it seems so difficult, the sequence of things escapes you, the snow grabs your edges or slips from beneath, the falls are exhausting. What enables you to learn? It's simple: desire. Twenty years later I sat in a small hotel in Wengen listening to Ingemar Stenmark, a Swedish idol if there ever was one—it is not an unknown breed—talk about his career. He was unmistakable in a race. He came down as if he owned the course, in powerful gulps and with incredible authority, slamming the poles aside with his shoulder as if he were batting balls. He had fallen in the slalom that day, which was rare—he was twenty-five years old and nearing the end of his career but still skiing as if everything in the world depended on it. He was asked, among other things, what he felt had given him his greatness. "Desire," he said, and added, "I don't think I have talent to an extraordinary degree." It was desire and work, he said, as one of the rewards, a tall blonde, came in and put his running jacket on the couch beside him in preparation for supper..

You continue to try. This snow is windswept, the instructor explains. This is called marble. This is called powder. Follow me closely, he says, as if you can, turn where I turn. Trying to do what he does, forgetting some things, remembering others, somehow you follow. The trail is narrowing, you are going faster than you should and farther, beyond your endurance. Suddenly he swings against the slope, comes to a stop, and looks back as astonishingly you do the same. "*Jawohl!*" The sweetness of that word.

One morning you wake unaware that, mysteriously, something has changed. This day it comes to you, the ability to slip where he slips, to turn where he turns, to begin to imitate the set of his shoulders, the resilience of his knees. All day, run after run, filled with an immense, unequaled happiness, and at the end into town together, down the last, easy slopes, and so weary that you fall asleep after supper in your ski clothes, the lights burning throughout the night.

*

In April we skied again and afterward went down to Venice. The Gritti was inexpensive then. The floors were marble and the hallways lit by lanterns held by gilt Moorish hands. Anyway you can say you've been there. In fact it was dull. We drove back through Udine and Cortina. I was thinking about the following year and asked the prices. Room, bath, and demi-pension in season was 3,600 lire, at the time about $6.

We never made it back to Cortina. We skied in other places in Europe over the years including Kitzbühel and Wengen, where the big races are held, the Hahnenkamm and Lauberhorn, the classics, always in the middle of January.

Racing in Europe is a heroic sport, more popular than it is in America and far more rewarding. Huge crowds gather along the course, ringing cowbells and shouting Hopp! Hopp! Hopp! as the racers come down, and hundreds of reporters are there.

I skied the Hahnenkamm once with Toni Sailer. He was a member of Kitzbühel's famous *Wunderteam* of the 1950s, which also included Hinterseer, Pravda, and Molterer. Molterer won a silver and a bronze in the 1956 Olympics in Cortina. Hinterseer won a gold medal in 1960 at Squaw Valley.

Kitzbühel is a handsome town known for its skiing and unspoiled look. The latter is an inheritance of the centuries, but the fame of the skiing is owed in large part to the great racers who came from there. Sailer was the most unforgettable. In the 1956 Olympics, at Cortina d'Ampezzo, he swept the three Alpine events, the only man besides Jean-Claude Killy ever to do it. On the way, like Killy, he won the most famous of all downhill races, Kitzbühel's own race, The Hahnenkamm, a run of about two miles plunging through the dark firs of the Austrian Tyrol.

The Hahnenkamm is one of the oldest races, and indisputably the toughest. Characterized by extreme steepness at the start, abrupt changes of terrain and difficult turns, it is a course that is respected and feared. It demands everything, courage, endurance, skill, and like all downhill races, a little more of yourself than you are able to give. If you win the Hahnenkamm, you have done something. Even to race it is an achievement.

I was covering the race one year, one of the five hundred people occupied in doing it, and was trying to find someone who would take me down the course. When the course is open, any really competent skier can do it—I was looking for a coach or a friendly racer who could explain the details to me, the fine points only an insider would know.

"Why don't you go down with Sailer?" someone said.

"Sailer?"

He was running the children's ski school—just go up and talk to him, they said. He had raced in the Hahnenkamm five times. He'd won it twice.

"Sailer?" I said.

"Why not?"

I went to the ski school, which was at the bottom of the slope, not far from the finish line. There was a little booth and I asked for Sailer. He wasn't around, so I left a note for him, tucking it into the top of a ski rack so that his name could be seen. Later in the day I came back. This time he was there. Sailer was forty-seven but looked much younger, with the handsome, cold face of a man who has seen the heights. The note, I noticed, was still on the ski rack, unread. I explained what I wanted, to go down the course with him and have him point out its real features. Sailer was taciturn and seemed to show little interest. Finally he said, "All right. Meet me here at eight tomorrow morning. On second thought, make it quarter to eight."

At seven in the morning I woke, having slept only fitfully. Outside the window children were walking to school along snowy paths in the dark. By the time I reached the meeting place it was daylight, a cold, January morning without shadow or promise of warmth. Not a soul in sight. At exactly seven forty-five a lone figure appeared carrying a pair of skis. It was Sailer. He greeted me economically and we started toward the cable car station. A few people, among them racers up for early practice, were already waiting.

Sailer, in his red parka and black pants, stood there and talked to some of them briefly, the young Austrian boys—he had been one of the team coaches for a while. Then he sat down on a bench and began fastening his boots. Finally he took out two thin straps, which he fastened with some care above his knees. I watched this with a vague feeling of uneasiness. We rode up in silence. Out the frosted window I could see the bare, glazed course, partly hidden by somber trees.

The Hahnenkamm is especially difficult at the top and also near the finish. The women don't race it; they don't have the physical strength for it, the compressions where the terrain suddenly flattens after a steep pitch, or the fall-away turns. When a racer first comes to Europe all he hears about is the Hahnenkamm, the horror stories, "I was going eighty miles an hour in the fog," the terrible crashes, bodies covered with blood borne away on stretchers. Twenty-five or thirty thousand people come to see it, and millions more watch on television.

At the top Sailer put on his skis without a word and headed for the small hill that went up to the starting area. We sidestepped up. The snow on top was trampled by the boots of racers who in previous days had been waiting there for their practice runs. Now it was vacant. As we began to cross it I finally stopped him to ask if we could talk for a minute about what we were going to do.

"We can talk better at the bottom," he said.

He headed for the starting hut but I made one more attempt to engage him. How many times, I asked, had he skied this course? He thought for a moment.

"1952," he said, "1953 . . ."

"Not just the races. All the times. Counting practice."

"Those don't matter," he said.

The starting hut has no floor; it's set right on the snow. There is a railing down the middle to create a kind of waiting area on one side. Sailer glided around it and lined up in the gate. There he paused and looked down the bleak, empty course. They had been working on it all week. Difficult to know what his thoughts were, his memories. He first won the race the year of his Olympic sweep when he won the downhill, normally a matter of hundredths, by three and a half seconds, the slalom by four seconds and the giant slalom by more than six seconds. It was the greatest individual performance ever. Nobody, one authority says, has ever come close to those time differences, especially in giant slalom. Killy won by razor-thin margins.

*

From the starting gate the course goes down sharply to a hard left turn that leads into an even steeper, narrower pitch called the Mausfalle. After that there's another, the Steilhang. Sailer stood with the tips of his skis hung out over nothing. I felt as if we were about to step off a precipice.

He turned his head and offered something for the first time.

"How are your edges?" he asked. "Sharp? Because it's all ice here. If they're not sharp, I don't think you're going to make it."

Then he was off. I watched in disbelief as he made one or two confident turns and went out of sight to the left at the bottom. My skis were rented. I pushed them out over the edge. I had pictured us skiing slowly down the side of the course, shadowing it leisurely. It wasn't going to be like that.

I pushed off. From the first moment it was like a car without brakes. On the frozen surface my edges wouldn't hold. I tried to turn, but the skis only clattered. Picking up speed, I couldn't make the last turn, fell and got up quickly. Sailer was standing at the top of the Mausfalle.

"The ice isn't bad," he commented as I reach him, "it's grippy."

When he was racing they used to pre-jump here and go most of the way down in the air. Now they press, holding their skis on the ground and taking the air as it comes. At the bottom it flattens suddenly—it's called a compression— driving the legs up into the body. There's no time for recovery. Three quick turns lead into the Steilhang, more difficult still. These turns are very important, Sailer commented, you have to make them correctly to keep up maximum speed. I nodded reluctantly.

On the Steilhang is something unexpected: Austrian ski troops at work grooming the course. They are under the supervision of Willy Schaeffler, a former United States ski team coach now in his sixties. I know Schaeffler and am relieved to see him.

"What are you doing here?" he says.

We're stopped beside him. "Toni's showing me the Hahnenkamm," I say casually.

"Him? He doesn't know anything about the Hahnenkamm," Schaeffler says, to my alarm. "He's forgotten it all."

He laughs at his own joke.

Sailer says nothing. After a moment, merely, "Let's go."

He lets his skis run down the rest of the Steilhang, some twenty or thirty yards, onto a relatively flat road through the woods. It feels like we are going sixty miles an hour. We are probably doing twenty. The tension is beginning to ease, however. The top part is the hardest—perhaps we're going to make it.

We come to another pitch, not so steep. It's called the Alteschneise—the Old Cut—and is where Sailer fell in 1958. He points to the approximate spot. He hit a fast place or bump, he doesn't know which—the course was narrower and rougher then—and the skis just went out from under him.

He lets slip a pronouncement of, up to that point, record length. "You're skiing very well," he says. I may have been—I didn't feel it. I felt like the boxer who has a cold bucket of water thrown on him and hears someone say, "Wake up, you won the fight." I also felt lucky he hadn't seen me go down on a hand and knee at the first turn on top.

Through the middle section it is relatively pleasant, the sort of terrain that lets you ski fast but doesn't oblige you to. And it's less icy.

Ahead is the last pitch. It's the final test of the race and has a brutal compression at the bottom, where many racers have fallen and more than a few have ended their careers. Just before reaching it we see someone else on the course, a stocky figure in a blue ski suit who is gazing down the mountain almost pensively. It's the Austrian coach, Kahr, known as Downhill Charlie—the Austrians have a proprietary feeling toward the event they regard as their exclusive domain. Kahr and Sailer exchange a few quiet words like a couple of fishermen. The sun has just come up and is casting a shadow down at the bottom where, Kahr points out, the racers will be at their maximum speed, eighty-five or ninety miles an hour. One thing the two of them agree on—the snow is perfect.

We go down the last steep pitch together. It's challenging but fairly wide. There is room to turn, and the compression is nothing because we cross it at an angle and at reasonable speed. The long straightaway to the finish is like applause.

True to his word, in a little restaurant at the foot of the slope Sailer talks about racing, what it was to be a racer, what it takes to win. There are things you can learn from the coaches and things you can't learn. "Guts," he comments, "Will."

We talk for half an hour. He seems very different here, almost amiable. He was the son of a roofer. He became a great champion, knew all the glamour, and now is back in his home town. They are cheering for others now. When he looks back on it, the races, the fame, the records that probably will never be equaled, when he looks back on all of that, what does he think of? He reflects for a moment.

"Well, I think it was a good thing to do it. Sport makes character," he says.

I walk back to the hotel. It's barely nine o'clock. The early skiers are walking past me toward the cable car. The day is beginning to take on winter brilliance, the snow sparkling, faces animated and bright.

"Did you do it? Did you go down with Sailer? How was it?"

It will be true one day even if it isn't now. "The greatest run of my life," I say and go upstairs and back to bed.

*

A Frenchman I sat next to once on a plane joined me, out of sheer boredom probably, in a discussion about life. To throw him off I took the position that life in Europe, in his own country in particular, was in many ways better than life in the United States, a perhaps exuberant view but I was just seeing how things would go. "The bread is better," I said.

"The bread? Yes, perhaps."

"The food is better," I continued. He shrugged and almost at the same time nodded a little. Between us there was the tone of men comparing wives. "The attention to the details of life," I said.

"Yes, yes," he said, "but the United States has given something more important to the world. The modern world would not exist without it."

"What's that?"

"They invented credit."

Plastic. It applies to more than credit cards. There was a time before the advent of crowds, when Europe was not awash in money—in fact when there was something of a drought—when ski boots were made of leather, often to order and delivered within two or three days. They put your foot down on a piece of brown wrapping paper, traced it, took a few measurements, and when you came back, there were your boots. That was the *ancien régime*. Karl Molitor, who lives in Wengen, in Switzerland, had a factory and used to manufacture leather boots. He was also a racer and had an idea of what a boot should be. He raced in the Lauberhorn, of course, which is above Wengen, and as with Sailer I once went down the course with him on a *besichtigung*, as he said, a reconnaissance. Accompanying us was a beautiful Swiss woman in a close-fitting ski suit. I never quite understood what relationship she had to the course or to Molitor, but I accepted it as part of national enthusiasm for the race, which is of such dimension that if a Swiss wins there is no closing time for the bars.

You reach the start of the course by taking the train from Wengen up to Kleine Scheidegg, and then a ski lift. The Lauberhorn is a very long race, about 2.7 miles, some 30 percent longer than most races, and it has, as one racer explained, everything: changes in terrain, difficult turns, steepness in places, and the hardest part at the end. "You have to pace yourself more," he said, "decide how much you can give." This makes it more strategic than a simple all-out assault.

The morning we skied was the day of the race, and we were allowed on because Molitor was the chief of the course. At the time he was in his early sixties, though he appeared at least ten years younger. It had snowed; there was a cold, fresh layer on the ground, the first snow in several weeks. Molitor took a turn or two in it. "The snow's too good for racing," he commented approvingly as we started down.

The beginning was gradual. The first big pitch is the Dog's Head—the racers would be in the air here, Molitor called out. The turns before the bridge, he said a little later, were critical. "You can lose more time on the slow part than you can gain on the fast."

The most famous feature is a place on the course called the Austrian Hole, where one year the entire Austrian team crashed. Finally there is a last, steep schuss, not particularly long, but thought-provoking. "No turns here," Molitor warned; this was to avoid any marring of the surface. I watched him go down, then the Swiss woman. Then I went. It felt fast.

Molitor had won the race six times, he admitted. When was that, I asked?

"A hundred years ago," he said carelessly.

Later that day I watched the race. There was a mist—actually thin, low-hanging clouds on the upper part of the course, out of which the racers shot in their skin-tight suits, past crowds and black trees, flying in the air at top speed, curving around crucial turns. As it happened, the bars didn't stay open late; an Austrian won that year.

*

For several weeks before the 1968 Winter Olympics in Grenoble, Robert Redford—who was to be the star of *Downhill Racer*, the movie we were working on—and I travelled with the U.S. Ski Team, taking in the daily routine and avidly listening to conversations, in defiance of Matisse's famous dictum that exactitude is not truth. The most visible and important figure on the team was Billy Kidd; there were hopes he would win the downhill or slalom. He was from New England, a region of damp, bitter winters and often icy runs. I saw him and the associated bleakness as being the right thing for the movie's hero. I never had an opportunity to talk much to Kidd, who was either arrogant or shy, possibly both, but I had worked it all out in my mind and one night at dinner explained it to Redford.

He shook his head, No, not Kidd, he had someone else in mind.

"Who?"

"At the end of the table there."

He was referring to a blond, virtually unacknowledged member of the team whose principal distinction, as far as I could tell, was the number of times he boasted he had broken his leg. His same was Spider Sabich. Like Redford he was from California, and I realized that Redford had singled him out because he saw in him a type he knew very well: himself.

Over the next few years I got to know Sabich and it became obvious that Redford's judgment was good: he was an admirable man. He raced professionally; in fact he was largely responsible for the popularity of professional ski racing and became its world champion, a somewhat dubious title, but like Redford he had achieved stardom. (Redford did not become a star because of *Downhill Racer*. Against advice from his agent he grew a mustache to play the Sundance Kid opposite Paul Newman, and it was this that did the trick.) Sabich was not as lucky with his own costar, Claudine Longet, who during an argument and out of jealousy shot and killed him one day in Aspen. Sabich had made a business of winning, often by the smallest margin, and it was by a very small margin that he died—Longet had shot him with a .22 pistol, which ordinarily would not have done much damage, but the bullet nicked the aorta and he bled to death before anything could be done.

*

I went to Aspen to ski the first time in 1959 and immediately broke my arm, though that did not color my impressions. There were two doctors in town at that time, neither of them millionaires, and you did not have to have an appointment. One of them put the arm in a cast, and I went back to skiing a day or two later at lesser speed. There was also a fellow in those days who parked his car at the foot of the mountain and for the annual premium of a dollar would drive you to the hospital if anything happened to you on the slopes. In short, it was cozy.

When we moved there about ten years later, they had paved the streets but dogs still walked across as if they owned them and sometimes sat down to meditate in an intersection.

The early glory of Aspen had been intense but brief. The town was born in 1878 and from the beginning flourished, but with the collapse of silver in 1893 there was a long, slow decline like that of a car abandoned in a field—the seats disappear, the steering wheel, the tires and doors; finally there is only a rusted skeleton, even the engine gone. In the same manner the wooden houses of Aspen, the streetcar lines and hotels, melted away.

The old crowd, members of the generation that was born in town after the silver boom, was still around at the end of the 1960s, though thinned by adversity and the years. A bartender I knew took me around to the office of one of the heirs to a great Aspen mining fortune. He was one of two brothers who had owned a renowned mine, the Smuggler, as well as others. When we arrived he was wearing a pearl grey, wrinkled suit, a white shirt with the collar points askew, and a wide silk tie. His pants, I noticed, were fastened with a large paper clip. He wore a hat on the side of his head and there was an aroma in the air of tobacco and whiskey. "Rick," he said to the bartender, "you'll help me move some things out of here, won't you?"

The things turned out to be a huge horsehair couch at least sixty years old and a set of large matching chairs. We managed to get them down three flights and onto the street, where a truck was waiting. It was evidently some sort of corporate relocation. "They're heavy," we remarked as we struggled outside with the last chair. "You're lucky he's not sitting in it," said the truck driver, who seemed to have some knowledge of things.

Coming back upstairs, damp with sweat, Rick said offhandedly, "Is that all? How about the safe?"

"No, no," the old magnate said, "but you're going to help me unload everything, aren't you?"

There was no one at the apartment we drove to, so we left the furniture outside. Afterward he wanted to pay us. "How much do you boys want?" he said.

"How much have you got?" Rick asked.

"Will two dollars be enough?"

"Two dollars! That's an insult."

"Come on over to the Onion," the tycoon offered genially, "and I'll buy you some drinks."

The Red Onion was a bar from the mining days and one of the best restaurants in town. I don't remember now who paid for the drinks. The old veteran had very little money, it turned out. He'd been married to a girl from Leadville, and when they were about to divorce he signed his half of everything over to his brother so she wouldn't get it. The brother never gave it back.

*

We lived in the west end of Aspen, which was the old residential section. The town was still relatively indifferent to fashion. Skiing began on Thanksgiving Day when you came down from the mountain, face seared by the cold, unseasoned legs weary, and sat down to the most memorable of annual meals. Around Easter, skiing ended—in early April, when occasionally some of the biggest storms came.

When we lived in the East you drove for hours to ski and often waited in long lines. Skiing was a kind of pilgrimage. In Aspen it was different, it surrounded you, winter and skiing. There were the still-hot days of early October with the first white dusting of distant peaks, the nights growing colder, autumn ending, the blizzards and epic days, breakfast in town with exhaust drifting up in the cold from cars with glazed windows. The world was far away, in fact this was the world. To the south and west the clouds would turn dark blue, and a certain smell, like the smell of rain, lay in the air. Tremendous storms coming, the roofs piled high with snow.

There are days, months, even years when you feel invincible, dropping down the face of Bell, Corkscrew, Lower Stein as if slipping down the stairs, edges biting, bumps disappearing in your knees. The memory of it all will stay forever. You hate to have it end. You are slicing the mountain as if with a knife. Of course even on great days there is always that lone skier, oddly dressed, off to the side past the edge of the run, going down where it is steepest and the snow untouched, in absolute grace, marking each dazzling turn with a brief jab of the pole—there is always him, the skier you cannot be. Afterward the hotness of the bath, darkness falling, the snow deep outside, couples in the street downtown, the restaurants filled, faces you know.

There are dull days on the mountain and days of indescribable joy, the runs empty, the air speckled with cold. People come to town who've been given your name, people come to dinner—the winter brings you together, somehow you make friends. You become a form of guide. Ex-hotshots on their college ski teams, confident despite years in the city and wiggling their hips in anticipation, say, "Let's go," and "You lead the way." In a minute or two they're passing by in an approximation of their old form, still ready to compete. Skiing is a little like dancing, grace seeks to be admired. "Where to?" they cry. "What next?"

"Oh, let's go straight ahead, there's a run just over the crest." It's a narrow, bumpy chute, invisible until you are practically on it, and will instill a sense of moderation—for a long time it also had a tree in a very inconvenient spot. At the bottom when they arrive, you merely remark, "That was great, wasn't it?"

"What's that called again?"

"Blondie's."

*

At dinner once there was a movie producer, a charming man naturally, with a good-looking girl he had found in Vail. She'd been working in a lodge there. "There are two things I like about Vail," I acknowledged, but the talk rushed on, they wouldn't let me finish. Later she leaned over to me. "Tell me something," she said.

"What?"

"I want to know what the two things are."

"Two names," I said, "the names of two runs, Adios and Forever."

And so it seems—the years cannot touch you, the disasters roll past. Jack Nicholson reigns in the Jerome Bar wearing a baseball cap and an uncynical smile. He is king of the place and even the town, a new king, everyone around eager to be touched by his existence, young men in cowboy hats, doe-eyed girls. A page had been turned; new people are coming, the terrifying young, splendid in their clothes, men in their twenties with their hair gathered tight in back, girls like addicts. I think back to the casual days. On a bulletin board outside a place called the Mineshaft I once saw a piece of paper pinned among the FOR SALES that said, WANTED, RIDE TO THE EAST, TWO GIRLS, WILL TRADE ASS FOR GAS.

*

There was a woman I knew who used to ski every day, all season long, whatever the weather, whatever the conditions. She was born to it, you might say—her father had been a racer on the Austrian team. Tall and sleek, she was married and had two small children; I often saw them on the slopes. Of course, she skied wonderfully, a natural. If you were too busy to ski, disinclined, or away, you knew she was there nevertheless. It was a kind of pact. One didn't know the terms, but they could be guessed at—her father had been killed while skiing, caught in an avalanche. She was being faithful to that, somehow. Other aspects of her life were in turmoil.

One afternoon I was in Denver and the phone rang. A friend was calling to say there had been an accident, an avalanche, and Meta had been caught in it. They were all up searching for her, probing the snow with long poles. I looked out the hotel window as we talked—it was already dark.

She had gone off by herself, skiing out of bounds. Lots of people did it. Her husband had been worried when she hadn't come home at the usual hour. It was her husband who found her. They dug her out in the dark and carried her body down. There are people killed every year in snowslides in Colorado and throughout the West, but not always emblematic people, not always goddesses. Later someone told me that she died on the very same day her father had, years before. I never bothered to confirm it, but I think it must be true; I think it was part of the pact.

*

Times change and things change. It was a beautiful town once, comfortable and decayed. The winters were long and dazzling, no one locked anything, we were countrymen. Slowly it altered. They brought the cities with them and the cities' style. Meta Burden is gone, Ralph Jackson, Fred Iselin, Bugsy. Not everyone has died, but they seem to have vanished, gone away. Sometimes the old town appears again, for a few moments, and there, half-blurred and thrilling, it lies at your feet.

I gave, over the years, a lot to skiing, by which I mean time and certain broken bones. The bones have healed—I can't even say which shoulder or leg it was—and the time was not wasted. I say that because so much of it is remembered and what is truly wasted is time you have nothing to show for and cannot recall. I never went on the Haute Route or to the Bugaboos but the rest is part of me.

I was going up on the lift one time with a young boy—this was in Vermont long ago—who was about eight or nine years old. He had blond English hair and a nice face. He turned to me as one would to a friend, and, snowy world all about us, confided, "It's quite fun, isn't it?"

He was quite right.

Classic Tyrol

There are places one loves without ever seeing them, usually because they have been written about. There are pages that stir the blood. *Sizzling down the long black liquid stretches of Nationale Sept,* as Cyril Connolly once wrote of France, *the plane trees going sha-sha-sha through the open window, the windscreen yellowing with crushed midges, she with the Michelin beside me, a handkerchief binding her hair*...Very few writers can appeal to the senses so, and of course Hemingway is one of them. It was he who introduced me, I think, to the idea of long, secluded winters and the mountain villages in which, during the 1920s, he spent them.

Hemingway wove his cloth with names. The race tracks—San Siro, Enghien, St. Cloud. The cities—Milan, San Sebastián, Key West. In the late fall, he said, when the bad weather came, he would leave Paris with his wife and small son and go to a place where the rain would become snow, coming down through the pines and creaking beneath their feet as they walked home at night in the cold. He spent his winters in Schruns, which is in the Vorarlberg, the part of Austria closest to Switzerland. He wrote about skiing there and in the Silvretta, at Kitzbühel and in the Engadine. He worked on *The Sun Also Rises* in Schruns. He made me like skiing although I never dreamed I would ski.

That was some time ago.

It's astonishing how things change if you live long enough. Restaurants in New York that were absolute fixtures like Chambord and the Café Chauveron are gone and so are galleries like Peter Deitsch's, hotels, theaters, even stadiums and streets. A whole new crowd comes in and is standing at the bar in new places, arrogant and stylish. Meanwhile, schools have disappeared, barbers, doormen. One looks around for things that are still there, real and untarnished. One of them is the mountains in Austria, where the good skiing is, where skiing as we know it got started. There are two great places there in the Tyrol, the province just after the Vorarlberg, one at the west end of it and one at the east: St. Anton and Kitzbühel. They are the beginning and the end of skiing and in more than a figurative sense since St. Anton was where, in 1907, Hannes Schneider first instructed tourists in the system that became known as the Arlberg technique, the basis of modern downhill skiing. One of the largest and probably the best ski schools in the world is still there with about three hundred instructors at the height of the season, most of whom speak English.

As for Kitzbühel, it was a mythic resort of the 1930s and at the cost of very little of its charm has become the largest and best ski station in Austria. The medieval town is still there with its narrow streets and sturdy houses, the cable car is just a short walk up, skis over your shoulder and boots biting the crisp snow. A day of simple things lies ahead, sunlight, icy pure air, the exhilaration of dropping effortlessly down trails through the black firs and larches—these pleasures, as Colette said, that one lightly calls physical.

The Tyrol is made up almost entirely of mountains cut by small Alpine valleys. Much of the skiing is through upper meadows that have been cleared of trees. For a long time, until the eighteenth century, it was isolated and virtually pagan, and farmers on the inhospitable heights were exempt from taxes and military service. The people are honest, hardworking and independent, deeply rooted in their heritage. Tradition is powerful.

I learned to ski in St. Anton, at least I suffered my first humiliations there. At the end of two weeks I had learned something, mainly how difficult it was. The next year I went back and stayed in St. Christoph, a village nearby. With an instructor whose name I still remember after forty years, I felt for the first time the thrill of what it could be like and went with him down pitches at the top of which he warned, don't fall here or you'll go all the way to the bottom. The sweetness of hearing him behind me saying *"ja, ja,"* as I did something right was overwhelming. He was a country boy as many of them are, quiet and even-tempered, and from that time on I knew how to ski although I had to work fifteen more seasons before I came to feel that I would never be getting any better.

Skiing, like sailing, is a world unto itself. Its glories are nearly indestructible. It embraces one entirely. It is a journey that follows a journey and leads one through days of almost mindless exertion and unpunished joy. Though countless skiers have been down the trails before, it seems they are still unconquered. Often as you stand looking down some steep pitch you have never set foot on, stoically preparing yourself, someone else or a pair will flash by and start down on a line even more difficult than the one you have been considering, doing it in short, expert turns and suddenly giving you the confidence to do the same, now, before the mountain recovers itself, so to speak. And then miraculously, down the fall line, finding the rhythm, leaving everything behind, the slope vanishing like silk beneath your skis—the hardest part is over. The sense of triumph is overwhelming.

*

It would be perfect if it were not for the crowds but except in cross-country skiing, these you find everywhere now and with them the cars that choke all civilization. The days of meeting woodcutters in mountain towns and staying at undiscovered hotels for the winter are over; the disillusioned, less prosperous Europe of between the wars will not come back. Filled with people as it is, the Tyrol still has three great virtues: It is beautiful, friendly, and cheap. Rooms, meals, lift tickets, taxis, discothèques all cost about half of what they are in the States.

In the hotels, especially in the older ones, the rooms are clean and comfortable and the linen crisp. There are still large staffs. They are young, most of them, waiters and busboys. In the off-hours they are usually sitting in the kitchen or in a room just outside it. The external relationships exist. At the front desk a couple of years ago a tall, well-made girl was working. She was from another town. She wore flowered dresses and her hair was done with the careful elegance of cheap magazines. From the office she was visible to the owner, seated at his desk. He could see her reach back for a key or lean over to read a bus schedule on the counter. He kept the door ajar and pretended to be at work. Occasionally he would find some reason to admonish her. He was forty, the age of longing.

The Tyrol used to be much larger but the southern part was ceded to Italy after the First World War. In their hearts the Austrians have never given up the lost portion. Almost all of them have relatives there, and many still own land or houses. South Tyrol is wine-growing country, and when you have a bottle of wine in Kitzbühel or St. Anton they call it "our wine."

It was the English who discovered the Tyrol and, as they did in so many other places, first made it fashionable. Since the last war and the waning of their fortunes they have retreated and been replaced by the Germans, many of them from around Munich, which, with the fine new roads, is just a few hours to the north. A few English are still around, of course, with their distinctive faces and pale complexions. There is a certain class of them that never changes. I was sitting in the bar one evening when a young English couple came in. She was wearing a tight cloche hat. She had a wide jaw and eyes with a lot of mascara, very striking. She was talking about the Austrians and right away she used the word "enigma" several times. She wasn't just a mannequin, you see. She had her own ideas and expressed them in a clear voice, the way the English do, as if their language as well as their customs were impenetrable.

You like Kitzbühel for many reasons. One is the feel of it.
Like ancient sea beds it is made up of many layers. There are
the fashionable visitors from Munich and Vienna, the French
and English, the families, the single men who are there for
the winter. There is the center of town with all its activity,
the sporting goods shops, boutiques, Café Praxmair, the large
hotels, the sled ponies waiting patiently beneath their blankets, frozen breath rising slowly above their heads. But there
are also the small, cozy pensions lost in the snow, with their
rooms, as Proust said, whose odors indicate a whole secret
system of life. There are the quiet hotels up by the cable
car—the Alpina and Hahnenhof—the many moderately
priced places like the Eggerwirt, the Tyrol and the Klausner,
at the railway station. Kitzbühel lies in a large loop of track
that carries, along with more ordinary trains, the Arlberg
Express, which stops at St. Anton, Innsbruck and here on its
way down from the Channel and Paris. Unfortunately it
reaches Kitzbühel in the afternoon when you are up on the
mountain. There are not many things as evocative as the
sound of a crack train passing the hotel at night. It is something distinctly European that simply does not exist at home,
like cathedrals, concierges, and currency exchange. If you
have never known it, your life is the poorer.

The vast, linked system of ski runs and lifts covers two separate mountains, the Hahnenkamm on one side and the Horn
on the other. The Horn has easier runs and fewer people. The
Hahnenkamm, for which the most famous downhill race in the
world is named—it is held here every year in January as part of
the World Cup—has lift connections with a number of neighboring mountains as well, and some unforgettable runs that go

for miles, like the Fleck, and end up in other villages from which the return is by bus or taxi.

St. Anton is somewhat different. Like Wimbledon or St. Andrews, it is nearly a shrine. Smaller than Kitzbühel, it has only about seventeen hundred inhabitants though in the winter it seems the whole world is there. There are many who are learning to ski, others who ski very well and some who return every year. So it has great crowds, animation, the Post Hotel, and some of the most demanding runs in Europe. It is higher up than Kitzbühel, though not high by the standards of the American West, and has a greater vertical drop. The Galzig and the Valluga rise above with their classic runs, and there is the Grampen which is somewhat easier. Around the corner from all this, as it were, is St. Christoph, consisting mostly of hotels. The lifts connect to the St. Anton network. Although it is a village that was a haven for travellers caught in storms on the pass as far back as the fifteenth century, St. Christoph does not possess either the style or the charm of St. Anton but does have excellent skiing and fewer people.

There is New York in winter, crowded and cold, *narrow and tall on all sides, full of traffic, accident, commerce and adultery,* as Delmore Schwartz described it, *its belly veined with black subways, its towers and bridges grand, numb, and without meaning.* Only hours away in this new age, a night's doze across the ocean, and you are driving out of Zurich in the morning, in the winter silence, the trees white in the fog. Soon you enter a different world, calm and unchanging, barns with stones on the roof, towns built around churches. Roads lead off through the snowfields to distant farmhouses, their serenity lasting through generations.

Man occasionally makes something beautiful, God nearly always. It seems that these mountains are like that. The ski towns lie at the foot of them, coming to life in the dusk. Tomorrow you will be kicking off your bindings after the last run of the day, legs weary, lungs and soul purged, and trudging slowly downhill to comfort that is like a timeless dream of home. Then there is the next day and the day after that and on and on until two weeks are up, or three, and suddenly it's time to leave, that soon. People are driving into town as you depart, fresh faces glimpsed through the windshield, those for whom it is just beginning.

"And we'll do all that and Saint Moritz, too?" someone in Hemingway says.

"Saint Moritz? Don't be vulgar. Kitzbühel you mean. You meet people like Michael Arlen at Saint Moritz."

Europe's Longest Run

Klosters has changed, of course. It's no longer the unspoiled village, two hours from Zurich and buried in snow, that Irwin Shaw found when he first drove down from Paris one winter in the 1950s. That paradise with its farmers, open fields and jewel of a hotel has almost disappeared. Its perfection doomed it. The crowds arrived. Buildings sprang up. But the skiing is still excellent, some of the best in Switzerland; the small hotel has lost none of its charm; there is at least one restaurant that deserves a couple of stars and from the highest summit you can still ski a long, beautiful run, the longest in Europe.

The hotel is the Chesa Grishuna, its guestbook filled with famous signatures: Rex Harrison, Max Schmeling, Truman Capote. It's a hotel that deserves all the affection in which it's held. Reservations are made months in advance—people often make them for the following year as they leave. Occasionally there are cancellations.

The exceptional restaurant is the Walserstube, and the ski run that begins high above Klosters and ends (after some eleven kilometers or seven miles) far down the valley in another village altogether is the Parsenn. They are more sober in Europe about the naming of runs. You don't find the theatrics of The Plunge, Moment of Truth, or one of my favorites, Adios—all typical of the American West. But what Parsenn lacks in the drama of its name, it more than makes up for in splendor and length. It's the site also for one of the oldest ski races in Europe, the Parsenn Derby, which is not part of the regular European circuit but which draws six hundred to seven hundred racers every year, almost all of them enthusiastic amateurs, hopeful or no longer so hopeful, men and women, young and old. When the course went all the way down to Küblis, it took the best of them nearly twelve minutes to run it, as compared to something less than two minutes for the typical downhill race. These days the finish line is about halfway down the course near a remote mountain inn called the Conters Schwendi. It's still a long race, about four miles, nearly twice as long as the longest regular downhill, which is the Lauberhorn in Wengen.

In the early days, sixty or seventy years ago, the Derby had only a start and a finish line—racers went down any way they could, which gave the locals an advantage: they knew the shortcuts and speed-building pitches. Later, when there was marked course, they still won because it was leg murdering and they were used to it. The national teams finally stopped coming, and the Parsenn Derby became a kind of folk race with regular and senior divisions. The race begins at nine in the morning and, with skiers pushing off at thirty-second intervals, goes on until well into the afternoon. During that long period the course conditions often change— and sometimes even the weather. A man named Korbi Boner, who owned a sports shop down the street from the Chesa Grishuna, was the last one to win the long version of the race. He'd entered the Derby six times and placed as high as second or third but never won until that last try. His time was about eleven and a half minutes.

Klosters lies on one side of the mountain, Davos halfway around on the other. You can go up from either of them. From Klosters, the Gotschna cable car, the only one there is, leaves from behind the railroad station in the center of town. There's usually a wait, sometimes thirty or forty-five minutes. Once up, you are into the great open slopes above the tree line, with a variety of lifts all around. Above are two related summits, the Weissfluhjoch and the Weissfluhgipfel. The latter, at 9,240 feet, is the highest point around. A second cable car takes you up to it and the beginning of the Parsenn. There's no point in hurrying. The run is going to be long. You might as well linger up here in the pure air for a while, away from the crowd. In every direction, as far as you can see, there are dimly blue peaks—some of them in other countries, Austria and Italy. Emptiness, silence and cold, all of it glittering and white.

*

The first pitches, which are the most difficult, come at the beginning, down a kind of gully between the two peaks, but they are followed by moderate sections—runouts—and in any case can be easily done by the average skier. The Swiss rate this top part *schwer*—the equivalent of expert. The rest is all *mittelschwer*—not very hard.

Very quickly, at the end of the upper section, there appears an old patrol hut called the Kreuzweg where, as the name suggests, the trail branches off into various ways down. The Parsenn run goes around a shoulder to the left of a slope called the Derby Schuss, which is packed only on race week in February but can be skied at other times if the powder is good. At the bottom of this schuss is a deep ravine, once the site of spectacular crashes on race day before the patrol began the practice of filling it in.

About halfway down the trees begin, and not much farther on, at the bottom of a pitch, is the Conters Schwendi, a simple, barnlike mountain inn, built in "A 1931 D," as the inscription says. Wonderful coming in out of the cold to the rich smell of cooking, warm, crowded booths, laughter, the sound of glasses and utensils. You loosen your boots. *Suppe mit Würstli. Rösti* (the delicious, browned potatoes) *mit Eiern. Entrecôte garniert.*

Then it is down through the dark trees, their branches snow laden, the only sound the soft hiss of the skis. The run can be icy in here, but you go down through meadows and glades, over parts of logging trails and across wooden bridges on terrain that, though not difficult, is always varied and real, as opposed to the shorter, man-made runs that make up so much of modern skiing. Down along the snow-covered haying roads, down through fields, past the village of Conters, barns with the smell of manure and hay, down, down, often without a soul in sight, past houses and on into Küblis where it finally ends. You lean on your poles for a moment or two, kick off your skis and carry them across the road to the station. The trains run about every twenty minutes, and it takes that long to make the trip back to Klosters. How long did it take us, you ask waiting there, not counting the time at the Schwendi, forty minutes, an hour? It's not a tough run—for that try the Drostobel, which drops down the shoulder of the mountain off to the right of the Gotschna cable car, or the Wang, just beneath the cable and even more demanding. The Parsenn is merely beautiful, especially in deep winter, December or January, with the snow falling, perhaps, and lights on in the houses below in the early dusk. The heart of winter has always been best for skiing, at least for me, the source of its classic images and purest joy: the snow, the cold, everything frozen and bright, and the warmth of the fire down there at the end of the last run.

*

The main street of Klosters begins across from a huge gray hotel, the Vereina, and runs past the Chesa Grishuna, the railroad station, supermarket, glass and steel banks and small shops, ending almost a mile away in condominiums and hillside apartments. Bland in appearance, it has long since lost its village look. There are still barns and old wooden houses but mostly in other parts of town and they no longer set the architectural tone.

Across from the station and cable car is the Hotel Alpina, modern and one of the largest. Below, across the river, is the Silvretta, which, together with the Vereina is still among the best—both were built in the 1880s to lure the English from Davos in the summer. Also by the river is a big new hotel called the Aaba Health. Not quite so well-located on the road into Klosters is perhaps the pick of them all, the Walserhof, with a fine restaurant, the Walserstube.

Down at the other end of town and the scale, is the Wynegg, probably the friendliest of the small hotels, with a very popular restaurant. It is a favorite of the British—Prince Charles used to stay there in days past.

It was the British who popularized winter sports on the Continent, especially skiing, but they are a small minority these days. Most visitors to Klosters are Swiss, then come the Germans and finally the Americans, who make up perhaps ten percent. Almost everyone drives to Klosters, although it's extremely convenient to come by train, and if you are staying, for instance, at the Alpina or the Chesa, it's like having your private railway car pull into the station across the street. As late as the 1920s, in fact, it was forbidden to drive cars in the Grisons—the farmers blocked it. It's hard to imagine now, just as it is to think of the town without all its new houses, hotels, and condominiums. "Every simple plumber becomes a millionaire here," one of the hotel owners commented regarding the speculation, "every architect. In Switzerland architect is not a protected title—anyone can call himself an architect," he added morosely.

Still, it's like the old days to come skiing down the long, long run from the top, kilometer after kilometer of winter landscape, all of it snowbound, the houses in the valley far below, the trail running swiftly, endlessly it seems beneath your skis.

Immortal Days

A few summers ago, searching for dinosaur excavations, we stopped in a little town named DeBeque in western Colorado. There was a grocery store, an old garage, a post office, and a bar. No one seemed to know anything about dinosaurs although they had an alleged forty-million-year-old tortoise fossil, turned up during road construction, in the garage. "Why don't you go and talk to Armand DeBeque?" they said.

Armand DeBeque lived in a well-kept house at the edge of town but he wasn't there. We found him at the high school where he taught journalism. He was working on the yearbook. He was sixty-eight and the son of a man who had founded DeBeque as part of a land grant given out after the Civil War. His father had fought in that war. Your grandfather, I suggested. No, his father, he said. His father had been born in 1840 and was seventy-two years old at the birth of his son. In one leap the entire history of the state, almost of the West, was spanned.

Colorado lies in two parts. The eastern half is flat, part of the great, fertile heartland that feeds the nation. Denver is the last city of the plains. From its hotel windows, to the west, the mountains rise like a wall. These are the Rockies. Beneath the mountains lies the great reef of silver upon which the mining towns were built. Almost everything was done by hand in these remote locations—trees felled, tunnels dug, shafts and galleries timbered. Sometimes you find the remains of mines with weathered piles of tailings deep in the wilderness. On the way to Crested Butte from Aspen, over the mountains, there are several. It is difficult to imagine such backbreaking labors far from any road or town, but then one remembers the purity of the ore and the size of the nuggets that were sometimes found: in one celebrated case, almost twenty-one hundred pounds of pure silver.

Walking to Crested Butte takes a day. The path at the beginning, in the early morning, is narrow but defined. Gradually it begins to fade and finally, above timberline, to wander aimlessly through high meadows, though the final rocky trail over the pass is plain. The air is thin at this height. One's eyes feel dry; the skin itches. All around is wilderness and fever-blue sky. A friend of mine once encountered two women walking with difficulty toward him near the top of the pass. Jehovah's Witnesses, they were wearing high heels. They wanted to know if this was the way to town.

Beyond the Rockies, at the end of the state, are the shale oil lands, the mesas that run into Utah and north to Wyoming. Hundreds of miles of gorgeously colored, arid earth with occasional farm communities like Fruita and Palisade. Through this runs the Colorado River, which forms the Grand Canyon and carries water finally into Mexico and the Gulf of California. Water is the most precious thing in the West, more valuable than gold or silver. The minerals can be taken away and the land will remain, but if the water goes, there is nothing. Land comes with water rights out here and they are carefully defined and often fought over.

Yes, it is beautiful. It is still beautiful because it is young. It is open, vast, and not spoiled in the ordinary way. Things have been built on it but they are not overwhelming, the land keeps its dignity.

Until recently, about fifty years ago, it was a rather isolated place, provincial and more or less honest. I knew an old judge in Aspen who had lived there all his life. He had seen it change from a ruined mining town to a legendary resort. He wore old-fashioned clothes, lived in a plain house, and was rich from having bought up a lot of property for back taxes when it was very cheap. There was a woman who used to sidle up to him on the street in tweed pants and say, "I'm not like you. I've *lived*. I've had ten husbands, I've run a whore-house, I've lived in different places and seen every side of life."

Colorado is like that. It has never been anywhere but it is wealthy and now the world is coming to it.

*

All summer, it seems, we have been outdoors. Days in the woods, days up Hunter or Maroon Creek, afternoons by the Roaring Fork. There is hiking in every state, and forests and streams, but the scale here is different. This country will not fit in your pocket. The mountains soar up from the streams; the architecture is vast. You can walk for days and never see another human being or even a campsite. You can stand alone on the edge of lakes and in lost graveyards where the stones, less than a century old, are already leaning and half-erased. The weather is perfect, as it is all year, even in winter. A great mildness, the earth dry, the trees sighing. We lie in the shade in the soft, piney drifts and fall asleep, face down. We walk to the creek to fish. A brown snake, perfect and slim, withdraws in cool haste, coiling between rock and underbrush. It hesitates and, as we step closer to look, disappears like smoke.

The sun is going down, the tremendous sun of the West, the sun that whitens New Mexico and Arizona, that is worshipped in California, the sacred sun towards which even the sperm whales, as they are dying, turn.

An hour of coolness, an hour of slanting light. The yellow road machines are parked along the shoulders. The irrigation water, silver, is shooting into the air. We are driving. The road is smooth and black. A colt is galloping with its mother through the darkened fields. The green of the hills is fading, the meadows become like ponds. The mountains are blue and there is a gentleness and grandeur that fills one with awe.

This is the country where Oscar Wilde once toured, standing on the opera house stages in a velvet suit and reading *The Autobiography of Benvenuto Cellini* to the miners. They were more impressed by his ability to drink them under the table. They wanted him to come back next year and bring Cellini with him. He couldn't, Wilde explained, Cellini was dead.

"Who shot him?" they wanted to know.

*

The railroads that served the mines are bankrupt and gone. The Colorado Midland had a branch that ran from Basalt, near Aspen, to Leadville, through a tunnel at the top of the Continental Divide and then, on the eastern slope, across a huge wooden viaduct far grander than the bridge over the River Kwai. I have walked that route, following the roadbed as it appeared and disappeared in the high country. The rails are gone, of course, and even the ties. Only the embankment remains, and an occasional swath through the trees, filled with second growth. We slept in the woods the first night and by noon the next day were near the Divide. The roadbed was difficult to see. It had been erased by fifty winters, but up in the meadows in places the scars of old cuts still showed, and at the end of them—it looked at first like a pile of rubble—was the tunnel entrance. It was flooded. A cold, ancient air lingered in the darkness. The fourteen-inch timbers supporting the roof looked solid, but there was no way of telling if they had rotted beneath the surface. The water itself was icy though it was August.

Only a thousand feet above us was the crest. Why build a tunnel so close to the top? When we reached the top we saw the reason. The mountain dropped away steeply on the far side. It would have been impossible to build anything on it. There was no trace of the exit of the tunnel until, much later, having made our way down, we spotted it at the end of a field of immense boulders, some the size of trucks, that had fallen down the slope.

The viaduct, so beautiful in old photographs, was gone. There were a few pieces of timber lying on the ground, nothing more. Its elegance, its wonderful strength, of these there remained not a trace. I thought of the famous viaduct the Romans built across the Gard, in France, but of stone. Two thousand years old, it stands to this day, and to walk across the highest tier, far above the river bed, is unforgettable.

"Do you know the Pont du Gard?" I asked. I was with my children, the two youngest, twins.

"The what?"

They had lived in France, but it was years before.

"The Roman aqueduct."

Silence. They were searching their memories.

"How far do you think it is to Leadville?" they wanted to know.

The original miners came to Aspen from Leadville, struggling over Independence Pass, in 1879. The road has been paved and is two-lane now though not an inch more. There are places where a car can fall for a thousand feet.

*

September ends. The light is changing. The Sunday afternoons at the music tent are ended, the men and women strolling to the concert in their fine clothes, the students in shirts and Levi's, the dogs panting outside. The tennis courts become strangely empty, the crowds are no longer three deep in the restaurants and bars. The ranchers drive to town in their curled, straw hats and stand in the bars for long hours, speaking slowly, with the long, deliberate pauses of drinkers or those eaten by fury. Their hands are worn. They have yellow teeth and smoke unfiltered cigarettes. They would be rich if they sold their land and that is what has spoiled their lives.

I drive to Grand Junction, which will be a great city one day, the second largest in the state, they say. The sun is striking the trees of the orchards with a dazzling power, they shimmer and dance. High school students lie dozing in playground yards. Young girls stroll past the small shops and gas stations passing the housewives they soon will be—hair in rollers and beautiful legs and husbands in orange helmets standing near signs that say, CONSTRUCTION AHEAD. The emptiness of all these lives seems to rise like the sound of a choir making the country seem more beautiful, more time-less and sad.

As the days pass the light seems to become more intense. The nights are colder. The field mice leave the pastures and begin to come into the barns. The coyotes grow luxurious tails. In brilliant sunlight half-naked girls in shimmering gold come stepping out of the bandstand at the end of the field, batons flashing, and the football team of the University of Colorado runs onto the plastic carpet. The sound that has been present all summer, the sound of carpenters' hammers, grows more feverish, floats on the air. They are building everywhere. Colorado is changing. The sleazy Larimer Street that Kerouac sang of has vanished. It is now a tourist area with huge apartment houses nearby. Black glass and stainless steel towers are rising in Denver. The airport is international, and the air over the city, once recommended for tubercular patients because of its dryness and purity, is brown as dirt. On winter days it hangs there like a huge, inverted bowl.

But that is the eastern slope and far away.

One year I helped put on a roof in a valley near a town called Silt. We were high above the trees. There was an incredible view—distant meadows, mountains all around, some with snow on them, the glint of a remote silo. The sun

was very hot. The hammering had a powerful, almost narcotic effect that, combined with the blue of the sky and the
warmth, made me feel part of something mythic—the building of a house in the wilderness. The owner's wife, Darlene,
and her two small children stayed below in a tent they had
rigged until the house was finished. There was furniture in it,
shade, and an oriental rug spread on the earth just as, I suppose, in the tents of the Bedouins. I thought of the friend
whose brother had once come to visit and, unimpressed, said,
"If you took away the mountains, it would be exactly like
New Jersey."

*

I have seen the fall in Buena Vista and Taylor Lake, Durango,
Fort Collins with the great lines of geese moving south,
Crested Butte, and Eagle, but mostly I have seen it in Aspen.

And it is coming. The horses stand motionless these last
days, soaking up the warmth. Their coats have become heav-
ier. Even their faces are growing a soft, thick fur. Close up,
one hears a steady, calming sound, the sound of grass being
eaten. Carrying some apple cores, I cross the road to a neighbor's corral where we keep the pony. She eats them greedily.
Her wet tongue is rolling, saliva falls from her mouth. She
has a slight, wispy beard, like an old woman. Her breath is
dizzyingly sweet.

One thing, always the last it seems, remains: cutting fire-
wood. I don't know why I put it off, the trouble of borrowing
a truck, I suppose. Getting out the chain saw. As usual someone has failed to properly drain it. The saw teeth—well, not

too bad, I can touch them up myself or take them to Joe Borgeson who'll make them like razors for a couple of dollars. Joe Borgeson helped widen a side road on Independence Pass in 1934. He's on top of his house now fixing the roof. It's been sagging since he bought the place in 1915, he says. Colorado used to have a lot of people like him. Aspen did, too.

The blacktop turns into a long dirt road that leads to Lenado, which used to be a lumber camp. There are a few cabins, houses, a gasoline pump that doesn't work and, past all this, starting up Larkspur Mountain, the tepee of Cathy Lamb, who lives here alone all year with her little girl. Her sway-backed horse is grazing in the small valley.

Once past Cathy's there is nothing, not a dwelling, just a gradually expanding view as the road climbs and climbs. Distant peaks appear: Pyramid, the Maroon Bells.

In the forest only dead trees, standing or fallen, can be cut. The best ones, the sixty-footers solid and clean, are naturally by now a long way in. From a distance you sometimes see one, miraculously overlooked, but closer it turns out that, though it's only twenty feet from the road, it's down a steep embankment.

All day it is cutting, with the sawdust covering your face and clothes, trimming, and loading the four-foot sections. There are very few labors—gleaning is one—that leave one so filthy and content, for it is wealth one is piling up, well-being. There will be blizzards and nights of darkest cold filled with the fire's crackle—a sound that, by itself, means contentment.

Wood used to sell for $25 a cord. It now goes for $200 or more in forest country, and picking up a few logs when passing the lodges' big, luxurious stacks is something I have heard otherwise upright men confess to, like poaching.

Many of the old-timers are gone, but there still exist a few individuals who define things.

One I know, a former marine biologist, lived for years in a little apartment wedged up against the mountain before he moved down valley and built a house. He is lean, tanned, his limbs covered with a coat of almost golden hair. He lives surrounded by books, records, plants, a piano, postcards, tools.

I like men who can do things, who know the names of trees and engine parts, the meaning of certain clouds and shifts in the wind. I admire the knowledge that takes time and solitude to acquire. Above all, I like men who do not put possessions first.

He has climbed all the mountains around here, walked every trail, knelt to drink from streams. He's been married. He's popular with women. He entertains. But life does not hurry him. He sits down to it as if it were a familiar table. He works in the winter as a chief of the avalanche section for the ski patrol. In the summer he builds.

When the others have gone back to the cities, when the speculators are on the track of something new, I like to think he will still be here, rising in the morning to a day that is his alone, like Chekhov in his garden, intelligent, amiable, intact.

*

It is coming. One more unexpectedly mild afternoon. One more trip to Denver before the pass is closed. Sometime in October—it seems on a single day—the forests turn to gold.

The aspens covering the mountains become incandescent. Something is ending, pouring forth for the last time. The grass is silver in the morning. The trees become bare.

I remember, at the end of my own life's summer, the last real climb I made, the east face of Long's Peak with a far more experienced climber whose name is in the histories, Tom Frost. A vertical granite sheet, Long's stands at the end of a lengthy approach, beyond scree and glacial ice. For years the difficult central portion, known as the Diamond, burned in men's minds. Although it is done routinely now, it was past my ability, and Stettner's Ledges, which had been the classic route, was the way we chose. There's nothing too frightening, although in places the exposure—the unimpeded downward view—is chilling.

We slept on the face about six hundred feet up. The lights of towns on the eastern plains shone through the night. The ominous, vertical dark of the Diamond was off to the side. Orion rose and fell. I say slept, but one does not really sleep. The sky finally paled, resumed its blue, and day arrived. We finished the climb that noon. From the top of Long's you can see north to Wyoming and south to Pikes Peak. A great sky, clear air, the thrill of accomplishment. The walk down, which takes hours, passed like a dream.

*

We are waiting. The elections are coming, the wine sale at Harry Hoffman's, Halloween with its gorgeous costumes and parties, but we are waiting for something else. We are almost weary of waiting. It is time. And then at last it comes at the close of a day. Fading light. As if from nowhere, snow begins to fall. It forms a fine coat on the backs of the horses. It erases the roads. From Hallam Lake the faint sound of ducks drifts through the evening whiteness. We walk toward the lighted windows of home.

*

It snows all night. In the early morning the points of iron fences have a long, delicate cap like the ash of a cigarette. Smoke is rising from the chimneys. A single tire track lies in the street. The feasts are coming—Thanksgiving, Christmas. The immortal days begin. Soon the lifts will open, and from high on the mountain at the start of certain runs the town will lie, it seems, between one's feet.

I think of Europe and learning to ski. In those days, in St. Anton, I remember men and women in their seventies on the mountain, and it seemed an ambition, a dream, to ski the last winter of one's life, robust, absolved.

I skied once with a former member of the Austrian national team. She was past fifty and out of shape, she complained. She went like the wind. She picked the narrowest runs, the steepest, and vanished down them in a minute. I saw nothing that day, not a lift tower, not a tree, nothing except her distant back as I tried to hang on. At the very end her husband took a disastrous fall, an egg-beater, snow flying wildly, his body tumbling like a rag. He came to a stop and lay still. We skied up. He opened his eyes and she began to laugh. She laughed uproariously as if he had done absolutely the funniest thing in the world. She was laughing as she helped him to his feet. *Schadenfreude ist die schoenste Freude*—the greatest happiness is another's misfortune, she explained. He was brushing himself off,

"Ja," he said.

I have broken an arm, a leg, a foot, and a shoulder in Aspen and lain in many hot baths at three in the morning waiting for the pain to subside. Places where one has been injured never lose their hold. I get a strange feeling nearing a spot on Gentleman's Ridge where I began to slide down head first, on my back and accelerating. The names of certain runs cause the heart to beat a little faster, to jump. Down Magnifico, down Steeplechase, down Elevator Shaft, down through the moguls and untracked glades, a happiness drenches one, a happiness that will never end.

It is snowing in Glenwood and Vail. The snow is sweeping across Denver, across the plains into Nebraska. The long months of winter are here, the lights of town in the dusk, the blue falling on the runs. There are crowds in the bar of the Hotel Jerome. The huge windows are misting over. The young men who in an hour will be waiters are leaving to change their clothes.

It is not a life we are living. It is life's reward, beautiful because it seems eternal and because we know quite well it is not.

Victory or Death

I did my first climbing in Chamonix in heavy shoes and a pair of borrowed pants. We were living in comfort in a hotel. The real climbers, self-confident types from every country, were in campgrounds or up in the shelters. They didn't look handsome, they looked scruffy and hard. I learned what various pieces of equipment were—the shops were filled with them—and I heard my first sample of climbing humor. There were many Japanese, you saw them everywhere, they swarmed up the routes. One of them had fallen straight down past a British climber, who commented to his partner, "Seems there's a bit of a nip in the air."

We climbed the Index, the Piste Verte, part of the Cosmic, and the Floria, all of them easy and all faded in memory. What I do remember is the crowded practice cliff where we went for an hour or two the first day. It was August and hot. I was put into a climbing harness and fastened to a rope. A few words of instruction and we started up. Ten feet off the ground I began to be frightened. The sweat poured from me. I groped and fumbled for holds I wasn't sure would work.

Anguish and uncertainty filled me. I couldn't believe I would somehow get through it and it was supposed to be easy. That was what kept me climbing, that and pride. I certainly didn't enjoy it.

In its great moments climbing is an ordeal, and like most ordeals it has the power to bind one to it closely. When it is all over, you remember the triumphs, but they are broad, like happiness. Far more vivid, unforgettable, are the moments of despair. You are far up, two or three leads at least, in some exposed place with nothing beneath but empty air. Down there is the road, perhaps, with tiny cars and trucks going by. You are standing on very little, holding on to less, and you will have to reach out, get your foot on something the size of a knuckle, but you cannot make the move. You've tried three or four times and nearly come off, or you've already fallen and banged your arm and knee. You have lost all confidence. Your strength is beginning to go, as well as something more important: belief. Panic is rising in its place. The leg that is supporting you is starting to shake—sewing-machine leg. There's nothing to the left; to the right is only that little crack too shallow for the fingers. You've explored it again and again. You must have overlooked something, some kind of hold, some combination, but you cannot find it and you can't go down; down-climbing would be even more difficult. You can hear yourself breathing, feel yourself tremble. You are absolutely alone. No one can help you, and you would give anything, anything in the world to be somewhere else.

A runner can drop out of the race and stagger off. A batter can swing wildly, a tennis player can stop really trying. Even a boxer, at the highest level, can quit. The thing about climbing is that sometimes there is no way out. You cannot simply give up. If Roberto Duran had been a climber, he would have fallen to his death. I think it is this rather than the dangers, which are exaggerated, that makes climbing powerful. It is primal, and climbers who may in other ways be foolish, macho, or egotistical nevertheless seem to have one thing in common, a kind of earned knowledge of their own spirit—character, if you will. Of course, you must risk something for this, you must push yourself. Even at its most pleasant, climbing is a challenge. Without that there is nothing.

Difficulty in climbs that call for a nylon rope, nuts, slings, carabiners—climbing equipment, in short—is rated on an arithmetic scale, originally 5.0 to 5.10. The upper limit has been raised to cover achievements once thought impossible and is now 5.13 or 5.14. A completely inexperienced person can usually, with a little instruction, start at 5.5, say, and soon be able to handle 5.6 or 5.7. Beyond this it rapidly becomes more demanding. 5.11 is for arachnids, and 5.12 and 5.13 verge on the unbelievable.

There are devoted climbers who never go beyond 5.8. At the other extreme are the hard men, the saints and visionaries who live in Yosemite or Eldorado Canyon and climb three hundred days a year, doing long, dangerous routes solo, without a rope, far beyond where mortals can go. Like most heroes they are unremarkable in ordinary circumstances. They don their greatness. They simply do not acknowledge the possibility of falling. I once asked a famed solo climber if he was ever frightened when the margin of safety was down to almost nothing, and what he thought of then. At times like that he pretended he was only two feet off the ground, he said, there was nothing to worry about, and that usually did the trick. He had climbed the north face of the Eiger that way, alone.

Climbing is elitist, which is part of its appeal, but it isn't a sport for the rich. It was popularized in the nineteenth century by the English upper class and gained an aristocratic reputation, but the working class took it over, and in our country it cuts through all strata—students, doctors, physicists, romantics. All one needs is a pair of shoes and a swami belt: a length of wide, woven nylon wrapped around the waist for a rope to be tied to. With no more than that you can wait around at the bottom for someone with a rope who needs a climbing partner. It's like being a caddy and is a classic way to learn. Going to climbing school is another. But among the kids with endless time waiting at the bottom for someone with whom to climb are those who will one day be the champions of the sport, if there were such a thing. Climbing is above such formalities. There are only names that have risen above others, that have woven their way into the legend.

*

We came over the pass late in the morning. The blue sky was empty, the Rockies rich and green. We were headed for something called Monitor Rock. The road went on and on.

At last it appeared in the distance, high as if suspended, a huge gray object on the forest wall. It slowly came to earth as we approached, and grew smaller. We walked up through the pinewoods, the needles and dark soil dry underfoot. At the base the rock seemed to rise higher than a church steeple. Robbins stood there looking up. It was a long climb, he said. Some sections might be hard for me.

"How hard would you say it is?"

"Five eight," he guessed.

We roped up. I was a little nervous—it's easier once you're off the ground. He stood looking for a moment longer, then walked to the rock and started.

Climbing with an immortal. There is a lot of waiting even so, waiting and looking upward. He disappeared over a ledge. From time to time the rope jerked into life and a length of it rose from the loops on the ground. He didn't bother to have me belay him, not at the beginning.

One of the great solo climbers once told me that he was uneasy only near the ground. I understood what he meant— somehow it intimidates one, it is reluctant to let you go. When the time came, I began to climb. The first pitch wasn't hard but the second was. There was a chimney, quite long, and then a short, bare traverse. By then we were far up. I found him waiting just above the traverse, in a shallow indentation. "That's the most difficult climbing you've done so far," he commented. Thrilling words. They fell on an apprehensive heart. We were looking out over the valley. Above us was another chimney, near the top of which was wedged a large boulder—tightly, one assumed.

"Watch out for that," Robbins advised. "Stay to the left and don't touch it."

I nodded. As he prepared to start up, I was aware of something else: the wind was rising. There were suddenly clouds. I watched as he worked his way up, testing everything first with his hand. There were occasional loose stones. Nothing, or almost nothing, was ever kicked down by him, however. I stood there belaying him and watching the blue of the oncoming storm.

I met Royal Robbins for the first time in a sandwich shop in Modesto, California. He was composed, taciturn, and had a sun blister on his lip. We talked about his background. His father, who disappeared early in Robbins's life, had been the welterweight champion of West Virginia. Robbins wore glasses and seemed slight, but he made a powerful impression. He was then the most famous climber in the country. He'd done the historic ascent of Half Dome, solos of El Capitan, and scores of other definitive climbs. Pure, highly principled, competitive, he had over the course of more than a decade become the guiding spirit of American climbing. He read Emerson. He believed in character. When asked about that, what he felt had formed his own, Robbins said, "Probably genes. And the books I read," he added.

"What sort of books?"

"Dog books, mostly," he finally said.

As I started working my way up the chimney the wind was very strong. I heard him calling down to me from above, but the words were blown away and I couldn't make out what he was saying. He was probably telling me to hurry. The chockstone was looming larger. After a while I was just beneath it. It was about the size of a stove, and if it fell, it would go down like one. I was afraid to touch it, but I couldn't find a way around. I tried one thing and another. Finally, I put my hand on it lightly—there was no other way,

I needed it for balance. It felt firm, and by putting very little weight on it, holding on to nothing, it seemed, I got past.

By now the sky was dark. I was in a hurry, Robbins was shouting, the first drops were falling, and of course up here was the hardest part. I was a few feet above the chockstone and could find nothing. The holds were all rounded and smooth. I began climbing anyway. Robbins was calling to me, telling me which way to go, when my foot slipped. I couldn't find a place for it, and one of my hands was slipping. "Rope!" I shouted, and it tightened, letting me hold on for a moment in which I somehow found a foothold and moved upward.

When I reached him I found we were near the top of the first half; there was a large flat area above and to the side. We scrambled across to it. There was a tree, which alarmed me, as I was expecting lightning. Above were two steep pitches, and Robbins started up the first on its most exposed portion, out over the face. After about ten feet he came back down. It was too difficult.

"It would probably go," he said, "but it's too much work."

Meanwhile the rain had lessened. It seemed that the storm might blow past. He began at another crack farther in. It went up about thirty feet and seemed, from where I was standing, to go blank in the upper third. Above that, who knew?

"Are we going to the top?" I asked casually. It seemed we'd had a reprieve.

"You've heard of victory or death, haven't you?" he said. He had a slight smile.

The final pitch began with thin footholds and eroded hollows for hand jams. Then up a corner and to a slight overhang. When the rock goes past the vertical, high up, I feel it is trying to tell me something. Near the end I felt spent. I hung there gathering my strength. Finally I made it to where he stood. I don't remember what we said, if anything. We were on top. The feeling was sublime. On the broad summit, trees were growing.

Even the most difficult faces usually have an easy way down in back or to the side. After a few minutes of standing there we started walking. We crossed the entire length of the top, descended via a path, and then walked back toward where we had begun. Above us were sheer walls, smoother and more intimidating than what we had done. Robbins paused to look at them.

"These are real climbs," he finally commented. And pointing, "There's an obvious weakness there, if you could reach it." He was indicating a sort of flaky area several hundred feet up. "You could start up on the right and traverse over, perhaps."

There was very little there. The rock was about four hundred feet high, almost straight up and with few consoling features, although steepness alone, as Robbins told me when I first met him, doesn't make a climb difficult. I had asked him what did.

"Lack of good holds," he'd said.

Climbing is ego killing but also ego enhancing. The big rock faces are often some distance from cities and civilization, surrounded by forest, rearing up in deserts, solitary, grand. They are part of the wilderness, and around them are wound the most ancient and sacred myths. Climbers, in the words of Lionel Terray's title, are *conquérants de l'inutile*, a beautiful, easily translated phrase that really means those who are ready to give everything to win a scrap of cloth. Terray, who became famous on Annapurna, was an alpinist, which includes rock-climbing but in the context of mountaineering with its weather, ice, snow, avalanches—what climbers call objective dangers. He was one of the most appealing figures of a generation dominated by Bonatti, an Italian who accomplished what is often called the greatest alpine achievement of its time, a solo ascent of the southwest shoulder of the Dru, which took six days and had never been climbed before. There have been remarkable solo ascents since, notable among them Henry Barber's climb of Sentinel Rock and John Bachar's of New Dimensions on Arch Rock, both in Yosemite. In any but a golden age of climbing they would be called unsurpassable.

*

I never climbed El Cap, although I was invited to once, and I never climbed the Dru—sometimes I find it's assumed that I did, and there is a moderate route up the south face that, given the right conditions and companion, I might have done. I'll never do them now. It's been several years since I've climbed, and I've drifted away from it. I don't think I'll be back. One spring, early on, I climbed Tahquitz Rock up what the very good climber I was with called "the toughest 5.4 in the world." That was because it was the first climb of the year. It would be even harder now, and where would one find the time, the sunny days, the freedom?

So, as the poet says, I'll meet them later on. They'll be no older. We'll sleep on the ground or in the back of vans again or up on ledges in the icy dark waiting for the first light. Out on the plains the streetlights of distant towns will still be on and lone cars moving along the road; you wonder where they are headed at that hour, to roadhouses, motels, home. Above, in the darkness, is the summit. The rest is silence, stars, and the promise of triumph when day comes, a triumph more pure, more imperishable, more meaningless than almost anything else.

Roads Seldom Travelled

As children we were not taught to love Japan. In the newsreels little men were raising their rifles exultantly in the air in conquered Chinese cities, and cheap toys made in Japan always broke. Set against this were two thrilling tributes, *The Mikado* and *Madame Butterfly*, romantic and of the past.

Then came the war.

I remember going for the first time. We flew up from Okinawa—it was in 1946, eight months after the surrender. The country was in ruins. We landed at Atsugi, the airfield near Yokohama that MacArthur himself had flown into when he arrived as proconsul, and drove to Tokyo on roads empty of all traffic except an occasional army truck. The city itself was shabby and smelled of excrement. At night everything was dark. We were warned to eat nothing that had not been peeled or cooked, and a carton of cigarettes would buy a weekend. It was utter defeat.

Decades passed.

Together with my grown son, who had not been born when I was a fighter pilot—the envy, as I thought, of everyone who was not—I found myself in Japan once more. The old Imperial Hotel was gone. Every trace of exhaustion and war had vanished. When we arrived in Tokyo, having flown all day across the Pacific, it was evening. The traffic was heavy, it might have been Los Angeles or Queens. We were on our way to Kyushu, the second smallest and southernmost of the four main islands. We were joining a bicycle tour of Australians, four days late, as it happened. They would all be veterans by the time we arrived. I had packed, as if for a journey to the Pole, every item listed in the advisories received from the organizers of the tour. My son confidently took only about a fifth of what was recommended. It turned out he was right.

We slept that night in an airport hotel. It was too late for dinner and we were tired. The Tokyo Giants were playing on television. The first thing one notices about Japan, returning after long absence or arriving for the first time, is staggering expense. The hotel cost about ten times more than a hotel on my last visit and twice as much as New York. Early the next morning we caught a flight to Kyushu. We were the only non-Japanese on the plane, on which an obliging stewardess was taking pictures of several pairs of passengers with the passengers' cameras. After a couple of hours we let down for landing at an airfield by the sea, the city of Miyazaki just to the north. We were coming in over the water, with palm trees and steel light structures painted the familiar orange and white. There was a clear, empty feeling of the tropics.

One of the guides had driven up to meet us. The group, which had already been on the road for several days, was about forty miles away, resting its legs near a little town called Nichinan. We drove south on a beautiful sunny morning.

Yasuhiro was the guide's name. He had a bronzed face and a brilliant white smile. "Call me Yas," he said, using up a good part of his English. The road hugged the shore. There was blue sea on our left, and a Sunday concert on the radio was playing a spirited arrangement of "Anchors Aweigh."

After some fifty minutes we pulled off the road and drove down a narrow track half hidden by vegetation. Set back from the beach in a small clearing was a nondescript building with screened porches. It was a small Japanese inn, a *minshuku*—in such places the rooms are simple and nearly bare, separated only by screens or sliding paper walls. No English is spoken and two meals come with the price. Shoes, of course, are left at the door.

The Australians were not at first in evidence. The owner was sitting alone watching a baseball game on television, which he wordlessly interrupted to bring us tea. We sat on the floor and sipped it. Barely visible in other rooms and scattered outside, alone and in twos and threes, the Australians were lying about. The introductions were casual. There were five men and five women, including an older married couple. They ranged from their mid-twenties to fifty years old. If you've been on a tour you've met them all. There was a teacher, a male and a female nurse, a pharmacist, a secretary, an engineer. It was Chaucer. We met them incrementally as we gathered for departure around noon. They seemed taciturn. It was only later that I learned they were in a depleted state following a hard day of riding over what they described as "countless 'ills." The chief guide, whose name was Keiichi, was about forty, tanned and wiry, firmly in command. He could have been the leader of a platoon that fought its way down through Malaya in 1942. My impression was that he never slept.

Outside we were given our bicycles—ten-speed tourers, well-used, without saddlebags or emcumbrances of any kind. We got the two that were left. There had been a misunderstanding. For some reason it had been assumed that my son was a mere child and a smaller bike had been brought for him, but one of the guides obligingly agreed to ride it while the other drove the van that carried all the luggage. Off we went. Front wheel wavering slightly, I followed the group along the track and onto the road. My son smiled at me and asked, as if between schoolmates, if I was all right. I had never been on a ten-speed bike before, but I had a feeling that would be the least of my problems. I was fine, I told him. So far the trip was a success.

Strung out along the highway, we rode on the left side. (Traffic in Japan keeps to the left, as in England.) Soon I could see only two or three others. Where we were going and where we would spend the night, I did not know. Too much knowledge is painful anyway. It is in small knowing that one finds happiness, in that and in nature, and we were definitely on the path of small knowing. The bicycle brings one very close to the details of life—schoolyards with their startled and then wildly waving children, cats surprised as they emerged from alleys, rice fields, women returning from shopping, bridges, serene roadside shrines.

On that first day we had lunch in what might have been a franchise restaurant, with plastic-coated menus and fast food, but on other days we bought things, some of them adventurous—unidentifiable prepared foods, prewrapped—

in small grocery stores, and picnicked by the irrigated fields or on huge rocks along the shore, swimming afterward in the cool green sea, which I endowed with nationality and even a kind of special virtue: Japanese sea, sacred and unspoiled.

Kanoya, a small town that is on the map if you look closely enough, is where we spent that first night, in a hotel, the New World, western-style as it happened. In my room, I gave my legs a lengthy soak in a tub about the size of a folding chair and then lay down, propping them on a pillow.

That evening we were treated to a glimpse of Japanese life. The dining room was on the top floor of the hotel, and during dinner we were there alone until a party of eight Japanese came in. They were well-dressed and one or two of them very drunk. They'd come from a wedding, it turned out, and were continuing the celebration in the local equivalent of the Rainbow Room. After a few minutes, one of the women, good looking and in a classic black cocktail dress, got up and began dancing by herself. She did some jitterbug steps. It was as if we were not there. Then, unexpectedly, she picked up a microphone and began to sing. She sang several songs, handling herself with the aplomb of a professional entertainer. Members of her party were encouraging and calling to her. I then realized it was karaoke, the words to the songs were being shown on a sort of television console with accompanying music.

After a while, one of the men took the mike. He could have been in the blue-white spotlight in Vegas. When he finished, they tried to get one of the drunks to sing but he wouldn't, and the woman got up again. It went on and on. In restaurants and nightclubs, people suddenly get up and begin to belt out songs—the polite, reserved nature of the Japanese turned completely around.

Although I had brought along John Toland's book *The Rising Sun*, I knew I would not be divining the real nature of the Japanese people from descriptions of World War II campaigns, however well-written, or from stopping along the road every hour or so to buy a can of cold fruit juice from a vending machine.

Gradually, I confirmed my impression of the Japanese as stoic and hard working. We rode past sweeping bays and beaches with the Pacific swelling in. The road usually hugged the shore. In the remote countryside, lone women were clearing weeds from the side of the road. At railroad stations in suburban towns, hundreds of bicycles were stacked against each other waiting for their owners to return from work in the city.

Kyushu runs north and south; about 250 miles long, 100 miles wide, and shaped like an upside-down J. At the curved northern tip is Nagasaki, for centuries the sole part open to foreigners. At the southern end a great body of water enters, almost fifty miles long and fifteen wide, Kagoshima Bay, and near its apex is the city of Kagoshima. Like all of Japan, Kyushu is mountainous. The big cities and main roads lie along the shore.

Our route covered the southernmost part, the two long arms of land that form the sides of Kagoshima Bay. It was late May and the weather was hot. The rainy season was only a few weeks away. For the most part we stayed close to the sea. Unknown towns, roads without names. Japanese villages are very much like those in Sicily, another island of dark eyes.

Architecturally they are undistinguished and often defaced, if they are of any size, with advertisements and signs. The predominant color is grey. Still, there is a sense of tranquility and order. The open seacoast itself is unspoiled. Between the road and the sea there is only the rare house and almost never a restaurant or hotel. In towns, of course, it's different.

Usually we rode in the morning for three hours or so, stopped for lunch, and went on for three or four hours more in the afternoon. I never wore the yellow jersey that in the Tour de France is awarded for having led the group during the previous day's stage of the race. I never even tried to win it, a certain wisdom having come over me during the course of years. I should add that, in fact, there was no yellow jersey, although you could usually find the same faces, among them my son's, out in front.

Once, having started a few minutes early to go to the post office at the beginning of the day, I found myself out on the road ahead of everyone and, to savor the joy of it, rode as hard as I could for nearly an hour, looking back over my shoulder from time to time and to my happiness seeing no one. Finally, ahead of me, I spotted another bicycle and a moment later my heart sank—I recognized the shape. It was the schoolteacher and I was just catching up to the tail of the group.

Depending on the terrain, we covered between thirty-five and seventy kilometers a day. The pace was moderate although there was a kind of understanding that it was not good form to dismount and walk up even the steepest of hills—and some of them were steep. There were some of first-category difficulty and there were some, as they say in the European bike races, beyond category. Sun beating down

on the hard road, eyebrows soaked with sweat, the route
going up and up endlessly, past quarries, forests, past everything, with no indication of where or even if it would end—
these were some of the daily pleasures. You are standing on
the pedals and even then they barely move. The bike is practically motionless. No one in sight. Above you the road
turns. Perhaps it's the last turn before the crest. If not, perhaps the next to last. Is this a description of touring? Partly.
By now I have nearly forgotten the burning legs and mut-
tered commands to oneself for just twenty more strokes.
What remains is the glorious feeling of finally reaching the
destination, pulling out the bedding and lying down for half
an hour or so without speaking.

There are two kinds of Japanese inn, *ryokan* and the
smaller *minshuku*. They are similar: plain rooms, with toilet
and communal bath down the hall. You sleep on the floor on
a futon, a slim sheath covered in clean linen, beneath a down
comforter. In late May the weather was hot, and mosquitoes
were a greater concern than warmth. There is usually a low
table with a tea service, hot water in a large thermos, and
boxes of tea. Perhaps a television. Nothing else. Out the window there are palm trees and an empty beach, or rice fields,
or the back of a nameless hotel and a train. The principal
entertainment is the bath.

Every foreigner knows about these—Japan is famous for
them. The Japanese, it is said, have a genetic advantage that
keeps them from getting hangovers. They are apparently also
resistant to second-degree burns, which is what you will get
if you ill-advisedly step into the water without the interven-
tion of a maid or whoever is around to make it cooler. For

some reason you are not supposed to do it yourself, but this is serious and you cannot bother with propriety. The bath is for soaking, of course, not washing. Soaping and rinsing are done outside of, beside the bath, and the cleansed body is then gently boiled. The Japanese endure this for a long time. Until recently the sexes commingled in the bath but the custom is disappearing.

"Did you go to the Jungle Bath in Ibusuki?" a friend who had been on a celebrated—for him—trip to Japan in the 1970s asked.

"Yes."

"And bathe with all the women?" he asked eagerly.

"The women's bath was separate," I said. The room had been very large, about the size of a basketball court, with a high wall of river stones completely separating the men's and women's sides, though you could hear them laughing over there and talking.

"A wall?" my friend said. Dismay was on his face. Not even a decade and the fabled Japan he had known was vanishing.

In the baths the men held a small towel, like a bouquet, to partly conceal themselves as they entered. They brought their small sons with them, sometimes their very young daughters. One man had his two little girls, one of them about four, the other seven or eight. They showed no embarrassment or curiosity. They swam in the hot pool, limbs gleaming, wet black hair framing their lovely faces.

The food is Japanese, the hotels and inns are Japanese, the sea and sky are Japanese. We are sleeping on futons, with Japanese pillows. It's easy enough to become accustomed to removing your shoes at the front door, to washing outside the actual bath, seated on a small stool, and then immersing your body in water hot enough to sterilize bandages, but coming to terms with a pillow that seems filled with gravel is another matter. I eventually found out that the filling was in reality barley husks and that the pillow could be hollowed out, more or less, by well-aimed pounding so that there was a place to put my head.

I never really became fond of them but after it was all over I was fond of what they represented, an austere and traditional way, and for this, and also to impress those at home, I looked for the pillows in several Tokyo department stores unsuccessfully. On one of the last nights, I mentioned this search to a Japanese friend we were having dinner with.

"Barley husk pillows?" he said.

"Yes," I said. "I can't find them. Where do you buy them?"

"Oh, you cannot."

"You can't buy them? Then how do you get one?"

"Your mother makes it," he said.

For us, speaking only a few words of Japanese and strangely clad, gliding though landscape and lodgings, not part of either, it is impossible to know the people. The wife of the married couple, who was the teacher, had brought along and was reading a novel by Soseki Natsume, the first great modern writer of Japan, who had a profound influence on writers who came after like Tanizaki, Kawabata, and Mishima. My son was reading Lafcadio Hearn, the most important of the foreign writers to illuminate Japan for us. Hearn, insofar as an outsider can, became Japanese, lived there, taught at the Imperial University of Tokyo, and married a Japanese woman, the daughter of a samurai family.

One of his stories, of the life and death of a cricket, *Kusa-Hibari*, is as pure and haunting as anything I know. The country he wrote of is already no more but its spirit has not changed.

To a large extent I was drawn back to Japan by the quality and elegance of its writers, of whose existence I was not even aware when I was younger. Sympathy and admiration, however, are not sufficient to bring one to a real understanding of Japan. The obvious barriers, language and custom, are too wide. Feverishly pursuing western ideas and fashions in clothes, music, sports, eating, almost everything one's eye falls on, the Japanese are nevertheless separated from the west by a formidable gulf. Theirs is a unified, blood-shared culture. It is a culture that declines to be known. What is happening on the other side of the curtain we try to discern by arranging the details of a journey into some kind of coherence, but the arrangement is our own and hastily put together. The true pattern and depth eludes us. The stunning final act of Mishima's life we are able to describe and even in a sense to understand but its impulse remains incomprehensible.

We bicycled for a week, staying in places like Sata, faintly renowned because the thirty-first parallel crosses the cape just south of it, and Ibusuki, with its hot therapeutic sands and instruction cards in hotel elevators warning of "earthquekes." From the window of our hotel we could see palm trees, the wide bay and the mountains on the far side veiled in mist, as in Japanese prints. In the morning there was the low, beautiful clicking sound of trains going by. We also stayed in Kagoshima, with its smoking volcano across the water, the fine ash filtering down day and night. Japanese navy pilots had trained here for the attack on Pearl Harbor. They came out of the mountains to the west, dropped down to rooftop level and roared over the houses and department stores on the way to the docks and blue water of the bay. In one of these department stores, Mitsukoshi, I glimpsed the new Japan: gleaming decor, fashionable boutiques, and a basement that was a combination of Macy's and the first floor of Harrod's, with food and drink of every kind and description brilliantly lit and displayed. The only things that were American were some cookies and a handful of California wines. Whatever you bought was quickly and beautifully wrapped, which is typical of Japan. In Tokyo even the department managers know how to wrap and willingly do so. I preserved the paper in a number of cases, hoping to be able to duplicate the wrapping, but although I marked the folds with sequence numbers I couldn't do it.

We stayed in a modern hotel in Kagoshima, commercial and with extremely small rooms. We had breakfast in a dining room on the top floor. It might have been Naples with the sun-silvered bay and its own Vesuvius, Mount Sakurajima. Before going into battle, the Japanese soldier classically ate rice, soybean soup, and dried chestnuts together with sake. We usually had miso soup, several kinds of fish, rice, raw egg (which the Japanese break into their bowl of rice), salad, pressed seaweed, fruit juice, tea, toast, pickled vegetables, and five or six other things.

The city reminded me of Italy in other ways—the crowds, narrow streets impossible to find again, countless small restaurants and shops. There are arcades and long, covered galleries as in Bologna or Milan, streetcars, and here and there a slightly garish, pastel building called a "love" hotel with awnings discreetly hung to conceal the parking places.

Japanese homes in certain cases can be visited through a kind of cultural exchange program, and this had been arranged. The two of us were picked up at the hotel the second night by a young couple in their twenties. They had a new car and a two-year-old child who was whining and attempting to get into the back seat with us. There were two other children at home, the wife informed us. Her name was Mayumi. "Do you like children?" she asked.

"Who doesn't?" I said.

Their house was in a residential district of the city called Hiyamizu, which means cold water. It was already dark. The streets were narrow and serpentine. We parked in a small space in front of the entrance, a space exactly the size of the car. The other children, a girl of seven and a boy of five, were waiting inside. I had vaguely expected them to bow and retire shyly to a separate part of the household, although travelling with their younger sister should have given me a better idea. We sat in a small living room decorated with inexpensive western-style furniture while the children crawled over our legs, across the back of the sofa, spilled things on the linoleum floor, and brought out books and favorite toys in an effort to gain attention.

The husband, Kenichi, worked for a bank. It was one of the largest in Kagoshima, with many branches. He was in a junior managerial position and got, as I remember, one day a week off and half of Saturday twice a month. He had one week of vacation a year. We made an attempt in the confusion to eat some of the dinner the wife had prepared and finally set off for a visit to her parents, who lived not far away. The thing that struck me was that we left the house unlocked and the children by themselves with instructions to wash and go to bed. Strangely enough, I had the impression this was what they would do. I thought of my own country, which seemed violent and dangerous by comparison. In Kagoshima, in the morning, little children of five and six walk unattended in their school uniforms along the streets and alleys, and on suburban roads girls in white blouses glide by on their bicycles, flooding to class like flocks of cranes. It's a different world. The buses and trolleys are undefaced, the people friendly and polite. There are few drugs. Families are tightly formed.

The next day at the hotel there were gifts for us from the family, including a child's grammar I had admired and a note saying that the daughter wanted us to have it. *Now we wish you good health and happiness forever,* the note ended.

We left the bikes behind in Kagoshima beneath a layer of ash, fine as pumice, and from there took the train. There is a poem of Kipling's, burningly romantic, about a galley slave who is finally freed and who watches in sorrow as his galley beats out to sea without him. *I am paid in full for service. Would that service still were mine!* It was something like that. I looked at the bicycles lined up outside the hotel—I would not be seeing them again or riding through sunshine and rain. On one of those days near the end I had found myself for some reason all alone. I didn't know where the others were, either far ahead or behind. It was cloudy and cool. There was occasional very light rain. It was one of the most beautiful mornings of my life, unhurried, smooth, going along the shore. I had no past, no future, I had surrendered it all to the empty road. On the rocks below, the sea was clear and green. There were small rice paddies between the road and the shore, weatherbeaten houses, quiet villages. I was singing as I went, at peace with earth and heaven.

The train, modern and solidly built, left Kagoshima at six in the evening. Suburban stations with hundreds of parked bicycles flowed by. The lights of small houses began to come on. There were rooms by the tracks with clothes drying in them, men in undershirts watching television on tatami mats as their wives prepared the evening meal. The roadbed was exceptionally smooth and the cars well-lit and clean. We slept four to a compartment with a freshly ironed *yukaza,* a printed cotton robe, folded on the pillow for each passenger, and sometime during the night we passed through the tunnel beneath Shimonoseki Strait that separates Kyushu from Honshu, the main island, on which Tokyo and Osaka are situated. That night also, sleeping, we passed through Hiroshima.

From Osaka, where we got off, we went directly to Nara, an historic town that was once, twelve hundred years ago, the capital of Japan. It is a town of magnificent wooden temples, the heritage of Buddhism's entry into Japan here. One of the temples, Todai-ji, is said to be the largest wooden structure in the world. There are two parallel religions in Japan, Buddhism and Shintoism, but they are not mutually exclusive—some aspects of life fall under one, some under the other. There are Shinto shrines and Buddhist temples. The temples and pagodas of Nara have been built and rebuilt over the centuries as they have been damaged or destroyed by wars, fires, and natural disasters. Apart from statues, nothing is quite original but nothing is new. In Todai-ji is a great statue of Buddha, and it's said that if you are able to fit through one of its nostrils you will be able to enter heaven. As an accommodation, an opening precisely the same size as the nostril has been cut in the base of one of the huge wooden pillars, and on the day we visited, children and grown-ups were lined up trying to squeeze through it.

Regiments of schoolchildren were touring the temple buildings on cultural visits. They were in uniform, the girls generally in some kind of middy blouse and skirt, the boys in a white shirt and pants. The students wanted to try their English. Urged by classmates, the nerviest came forth.

"Excuse me," they said as their companions burst into giggles, "what time is it?"

My son by this time was a hardened case. He found the Australians uninteresting and being herded around by a group leader oppressive. On the second day of the tour—I should have realized what it meant—he had cut the sleeves off his T-shirt and began battling for the lead on the road. He missed rock climbing, which is what he would have been doing if he were back home. At every opportunity he did pull-ups to build his arm strength, on the doorjambs of hotels, the awnings of ferries, wherever he could find a hold. He kept to himself and read climbing magazines on the bus while the guide described the things we were on the way to see. But the unforgettable image I have of him surrounded by Japanese schoolchildren who were somehow magically drawn to him and who squealed and tried to talk while he responded, his goodness betrayed by the expression on his face and the warmth of his smile. Perhaps some day he will return, under circumstances as different from these as those of my two visits, and see the country with different eyes. There are things here that simply touch the soul. We were near the grave of Ganjin, the Chinese priest who was perhaps the most important figure in the introduction of Buddhism to Japan and who supervised the building of the first temples. The graves of many of the famous figures of Buddhism are lost or unknown, but this one had survived for more than twelve hundred years. There was a greenish pond nearby with a few leaves floating serenely in it, and as we were standing there a big carp lazed up and put a leaf on his head.

Our guide in Nara was a woman in her mid-thirties, the wife of a university professor. The story of her life came out as we toured the temples. She had eloped in Nara. She and her husband were both teachers at the time and very young. Her husband's father had just gone bankrupt, so there was no money. They lived in a small room, six tatami large (tatami mats are about three by six feet), with a very small kitchen and no bath—they used the public baths. That was long ago. She had been married a long time, too long, she said.

"The wives of Japan are so busy," she later explained. "Dry out futon, wash their clothes every day, go to market *every* day, clean house. Very busy. I'm not that kind."

The day we left for Kyoto I walked out by myself very early in the morning. There was the sound of birds and the low, smooth rumble of a train beyond the fields in which a woman was already at work, almost hidden in the dense cucumber vines. At the end of a narrow street were the train tracks. In the upstairs window of one of the houses overlooking them was a lone woman smoking a cigarette. She did this with sudden, decisive movements, her black hair swinging as she looked one way and then the other as if examining the morning and finding it the same. Then abruptly she disappeared. "Woman is to keep," our guide had said—I think she meant preserve—"and man is to destroy. Japanese man is always fighting and killing. Japanese woman is very good at keeping."

Kyoto, about an hour from Nara, is the spiritual center of Japan, with beautiful shrines, temples, and palaces like quiet islands in the noisy, modern city. We stayed at a small *ryokan* in a lively district called Gion. It was on a crowded side street opposite a shrine. All day we walked the endless, rectilinear streets to shrines, Zen gardens, palaces. At night the trains let off thousands of passengers coming home from work, and the restaurants along the Kamo River were lighted like countless boats. When we came in late there was the click of tiles, the aroma of tobacco smoke, and the murmur of voices from the office behind the reception desk where the owner, who was a woman, was gambling with three or four men.

The *ryokan* was four stories high and relatively modern. There was one woman of all work, good-natured and accommodating. She had gold teeth in her smile and laughed readily. When we were bathing she seemed to pass by the open window frequently and occasionally to call out something. In the morning while the Japanese guests were eating breakfast in silence and watching the news on television, she would serve, coming into the small dining room and asking us, "Toast-o? Toast-o?" The bread was in slices an inch or more thick. Somehow she learned I was the father of the athlete I was sharing a room with and this seemed to amuse her greatly.

I still didn't know her name but the morning we were

leaving she came out of the kitchen as I walked down the hallway in the *yukaza* after breakfast and, grinning, said something to me. I didn't understand what it was. She began to pat my stomach and rub it, saying *toast-o* several times, *papa-san*, and some other things. She hugged me. The owner came out of the kitchen and was embracing me, too, rubbing my stomach and patting me familiarly on the backside, laughing, talking to me and to the other. My son passed by. "What's going on?" he asked.

"I don't know," I said.

Could they be from the old days, I suddenly thought? Do they know me? From Tokyo, the grey city, the pilot's city, days that were, the brilliance of nightclubs, debris in the streets, the mornings of waking in strange rooms? Unlikely. Even at their age they were far too young.

We took the Bullet Train to Tokyo along with hordes of schoolchildren. Fuji was in clouds, we didn't see it. That night there was a farewell dinner in an Italian restaurant in the hotel. Some of the group had bicycled through China for three or four weeks before coming to Japan and were now going home. The married couple was heading north, perhaps to Hokkaido. A few were going to Vladivostok to take the trans-Siberian railroad to Moscow, then to England. In the morning they were gone.

Mishima's Choice

A.J. Liebling used to trust ordinary restaurants in France that were patronized by two enduring classes: priests and whores. They both liked good food, he said, and both were sensitive to value.

In somewhat the same way I have always liked hotels that were the favorites of writers, not rich writers and not the Gritti, but writers with worn jacket elbows who were fond of the feeling of the establishment as well as the price. I mean to say places like the Algonquin and the Chelsea; Dukes in London—which was Liebling's choice in his palmier days, though it is a bit out of reach now; the old Inghilterra in Rome; and small hotels around the Rue de l'Université and Rue Jacob in Paris, where Cyril Connolly once knew the "excitement of looking for autumn lodgings."

All of these have or used to have the same characteristics: slightly frayed, cordial, usually well-situated. The management is stable. There is no fanatic dedication to perfection. The rule, however, allows for exceptions. Each place is unique.

Unexpectedly, one such hotel is in the capital of Japan. As is evident, Tokyo is not Paris, although its best restaurants, staggeringly expensive, are French and the subways may be taken without fear. The city is vast, crowded, and in many respects dismaying. Its districts were originally separate villages that over the centuries merged together but remained distinct. Many streets have no names, and others for some reason can never be found a second time. Traffic is frightening and cabdrivers hardened. There are skyscrapers, rush hours, and, especially in the business sections, many new hotels with identical rooms, windows not designed to be opened, marble reception desks, and lobbies made up of shops.

The Hilltop—the hotel that was Mishima's favorite—is a different sort of place. The first sight of it is unpromising. On a small, crowded hill about half a mile north of the Imperial Palace grounds, which is the real center of the city, are two vaguely modern buildings of yellowish brick. Between them passes a curving street along which, at most hours, students of the surrounding Meiji University walk to and from class. Japan is famous for beauty that is concealed from the passerby. It's difficult to believe that these undistinguished buildings, which might be taken for minor department stores on Wilshire Boulevard, contain an intimate and luxurious world.

Mishima, who had an odd, off-key taste for western furnishings, stayed at the Hilltop many times. He liked the privacy and comfort, the mixing of traditional Japanese elements with modern ones, the serenity, European beds, views over the city, and carpeted stairs. He often stayed for two or three days to rest. Kawabata, Mishima's mentor and the first Japanese Nobel laureate, also patronized the hotel.

Both writers' lives ended in suicide. Mishima was at the hotel just a few days before his death for a final meeting with his followers.

There are seventy-five rooms, most of them furnished in western style. A few tatami rooms—with the classic Japanese matting on the floor—are kept for those who prefer them. Some rooms have small, private gardens. Some offer a view of Mount Fuji when the weather is good. There is an expression in Japanese, *yojo han,* meaning cozy and comfortable. It also means, more specifically, a room four and half tatamis in size. Tokyo tatamis are slightly smaller than the norm, just as Tokyo apartments are, but a traditional mat measures three by six feet, and such a room would be approximately nine by nine. Very cozy, to say the least. The rooms at the Hilltop are generally about eight to ten tatamis, carpeted, and furnished with a slightly masculine but not heavy feeling—a little removed from time. There are small desks, wood-lined closets, and on the beds both barley husk and feather pillows, a mingling of Spartan Japanese and the luxurious foreign. Mishima wrote advertising copy for the hotel on occasion. Of course he didn't mention the hard pillows, which for the Japanese are commonplace; the hot water that is brought to the room every afternoon at five o'clock for tea; or the fresh cotton robe, new toothbrush, and comb that are provided each day. He may have mentioned the air, which has an extra amount of pure oxygen pumped into it so that it equals the air of the mountains. Negative ions, presumably beneficial, are also added.

*

It was a guidebook's description, "erstwhile favorite of writers and artists," that caught my attention and brought me by taxi more or less directly to the door. The faintest trace of kitsch was in the lobby, a certain elegance that had been learned from a book, but this did not spoil the charm—memorable hotels are imperfect. After a day or two my pleasure was such that I was eager to know who was responsible for it all. Hotel owner, for me, is a solid and enviable title. With due ceremony a meeting was arranged.

"Mr. Yoshida does not speak English," the assistant manager explained. "He understands, but he does not speak it."

We walked down hallways past respectful maids. Mr. Akiyama, the assistant manager, had been at the hotel over thirty-five years. He started as a janitor and rose through the ranks: waiter, then bellboy, desk clerk. Now second in command, he politely avoided answering questions, leaving that to Yoshida, his chief. We entered a small meeting room with a long table and wood-and-leather chairs. After a few moments the door opens and in comes the owner—indeed, more than the owner—the creator of the hotel, the man who brought it into existence, piece by piece. He is in a dark blue suit, a pale shirt, and a striped necktie. All the rest is Buddha, wise and amiable. I like him immediately—what a shame I won't really be able to speak with him. He's in his seventies, his hair iron gray. He knew the war and all that came after.

I explain how much I like the hotel, how comfortable it is, and how well I have been treated. He nods. I would like to know a little about the background. He nods again. For instance, how does it come to be called the Hilltop?

Yoshida says something in Japanese to his assistant.

Akiyama says something to him. In a clear voice, in perfect English, Yoshida then says, "It was called Hilltop by the Americans. During the occupation. It was a WAC billets."

"I see."

He nods. We begin to talk and continue for half an hour or so. It seems that time is suspended. His voice is low, soothing, not without strength. The story of the hotel comes forth.

*

The original building was put up in 1937 by a coal-mining magnate named Sato for the benefit of his workers. Along with the emperor's palace, some of the department stores on the Ginza, the main railroad station, and the old Imperial Hotel, designed by Frank Lloyd Wright, it survived the bombing raids of 1944 that destroyed most of Tokyo. There were then only four or five hotels in the city that were judged suitable for foreigners. When the occupation ended, Yoshida leased the building and began the slow conversion of it into a hotel. At the beginning there were some fifty small rooms filled with worn-out U.S. Army furniture, and the process—the cleaning, knocking down of walls, furnishing, gradual redesigning—took nearly ten years.

Mishima and other writers began to come. Yoshida's father, a noted professor of literature, knew many of those early literary guests. They came because it was quiet and sympathetic, and because in those days it was cheap. They felt welcome. "The spirit," Yoshida explains, "I took from the *ryokans* [traditional Japanese inns]. The rest I made as I wished."

By 1980 he had renovated the entire hotel a second time.

There were eventually a total of six restaurants, a wine cellar, and a couple of intimate bars tucked in here and there. The cuisine is Chinese, Japanese, or French, depending on which restaurant you choose.

The hotel has over 230 employees. They may not all be devoted, but the ones who are not seem to make themselves invisible. It's the kind of hotel where, if you ask a chambermaid for a menu, she doesn't tell you to call room service. It's like staying in a great house where all desires are gratified but freedom is complete. You can leave the hotel and almost immediately enter into the life of the city, walking downhill and in a few minutes coming to Yasukuni-dori, a crowded avenue in the publishing and medical district with bookstores, print and pornography shops, and inexpensive restaurants of various types, including two of the best soba places in Tokyo. Soba is a buckwheat noodle, preferably served cold. Picked up with chopsticks and dipped in various sauces, it is brought to the mouth and noisily ingested. A full meal may cost about $8, whereas dinner in any of Hilltop's restaurants can be more than ten times that. In season there is a further attraction: The Tokyo Dome at Korakuen, where the Tokyo Giants play baseball, is about a fifteen-minute walk away.

*

The plummeting of the dollar has made being in Japan a luxury, but the Hilltop is still within reach, and compared with many things there, it's a bargain. A single room costs about $100 a night and a double about $150. Room 503 is a particularly nice deluxe single, the sort of room that is welcoming late in the evening, and Room 406 has a private garden and is especially pleasant during the day. The people at the desk speak English. Some of them have been to the United States, sent to Boston, Los Angeles, San Francisco, and New York to study how hotels are run there. The executive managing director of the Okura, the most expensive and grand hotel in Tokyo, had been employed at Hilltop.

Yoshida, as it happens, has never been to America. He has visited Europe instead, making a trip about once a decade. He mentioned, as the sort of hotel he stays in there, the Hotel zum Storchen in Zurich—a congenial, but not luxurious, hotel right on the river—and the small lodges in the vicinity of Salzberg. "In Paris I stayed at the Hôtel Massenet," he said. "It has heart."

I never stayed at the Massenet. From an older Michelin guide I see that it was in the sixteenth arrondissement, which is the silk stocking district, but its listing has disappeared. There were forty-one rooms and no restaurant; dogs were not allowed.

I once took the owner of an historic but run-down hotel in Colorado on a tour of Europe. It was his first visit there, and we stayed at places I thought would stimulate ideas for his own hotel. We stayed at the Baur au Lac in Zurich, the Connaught in London, l'Hôtel in Paris, and—one of my real favorites—the Chesa Grischuna in Klosters. The latter has a wonderful restaurant and its own greenhouse, which provides fresh flowers for the tables throughout the year. It was fortunate that I didn't know of the Hilltop at the time. We would have had to continue on, probably stopping en route for a night at the Massenet. When certain people recommend a place, you know it must be all right.

Trier

Among the things I really travel for are architecture and food. I like to go places where I am certain of finding both of these, but sometimes I like a detour or two. A few months ago, for the first time in almost thirty years, I went back to Trier.

Situated on the Moselle River, very close to Luxembourg and France, Trier is almost certainly the oldest city in Germany. It was an important provincial capital in Roman times, known in fact as Roma secunda, a residence of emperors, a center of trade and the largest market in an ancient wine-growing area. When Rome fell, Trier passed into the shadows, and over the centuries there it has remained, close to a dangerous border, often invaded, but always prosperous because of the surrounding rich wine country and its location on the river. It is a bit off the main route these days and hence overlooked, but like Verona and Arles it possesses remarkable Roman ruins, including its famous gate, the Porta Nigra, so called because of the darkness of the stone. The wall that enclosed the gate is gone, though other important structures remain. A more recent one is the house in which Karl Marx was born, preserved as a museum.

Trier is small, with only about a hundred thousand people, unglamorous and unhurried. In the days when Constantine lived there it had nearly eighty thousand inhabitants, so its scale has not really changed nor have its surroundings. The cathedral possesses what is alleged to be the original robe of Christ, displayed only every ten or twenty years. When I first visited the city, there was a seafood store where we used to buy mussels—the first ones I ever ate, in fact. I remember the fine hotel directly across from the Porta Nigra and bearing the same name. Large, old, with a mansard roof and many dormers, it was like the famous hotels in Cairo, Nairobi, Quebec, that were emblematic of their towns.

This time, I had looked up the telephone number of the Porta Nigra in the Michelin and attached no importance to its now being named the Dorint Hotel Porta Nigra. The desk clerk spoke perfect English but there were no rooms, so we reserved in a small hotel near the station and arranged to go from Paris by train.

We left in the morning from the Gare de l'Est. The usual crowds, the black shriek of headlines, the trains waiting, backed up to the stops. The cars were new and without compartments. On the very tick we began to move. We settled down for the trip. The suburbs slowly vanished and we were into the country, rushing east through the beautiful villages. The sun was shining. Green rivers slept beside towns. I was moved, as always, by the order, the calmness of it all. Immense rolling fields. Fenced pastures. Furrows. Hidden hares and foxes, immemorial prey. You do not see the loneliness of the country, flying past, only its order and its charm.

In the afternoon we reached Trier and from the first moment, pulling in, I was struck by memories. I recognized the station, the platform, even the clock—I had been in a fighter squadron near here and we used to see people off when they were going back to the States. Nevertheless a lot had changed. There were new Mercedes taxis parked in the street outside, and the woman in the exchange booth looked at me with scorn as I slide some money under the glass.

"The dollar is no good," she said.

"No good? What do you mean?"

"It's falling," she said with pleasure. "It's less than three marks."

Late in the day, we walked down toward the Porta Nigra. The street was filled with doctors' offices and an occasional bank. Trees ran along the center of the avenue and soon, above them, the deep brown stones of the Roman gate appeared. I had seen it many times but somehow it still thrilled me. The largest and most important Roman monument in Germany, the gate is like a great wedding cake of three and a half tiers, nearly a hundred feet high. Across from it, however, the famous hotel was gone—it had been torn down in 1967, someone later told me. In its place was a new one, boxy, utilitarian, part of a chain.

It was my first glimpse of a new Trier that began just behind the Porta Nigra, a pedestrian mall lined with garish shops cheek to cheek that ran all the way to the ancient market and beyond. It was thronged with crowds, an unfortunate blending of the drab old and vulgar new so that the heart of

Trier now seemed like a huge shopping mall. There was even a McDonald's with its familiar yellow and red at one corner of the Hauptmarkt, the beautiful square that was given its character and cross in A.D. 958.

"It wasn't this way before," I said. "I don't know what's happened. It's changed."

What I had expected was a return to a youthful past despite the warnings of so many stories and books, and I was disappointed to find it gone. The next morning in the rain I set out to see what was really there.

Trier is not an obvious beauty like Bernkastel, a small wine town farther down the river. Trier takes a little time and patience. It is a city without especial charm, like Frankfurt or Le Havre. It looks better in the fog or rain. It needs to be discovered—you must go in search of its treasures; you do the excavation yourself. There is a cathedral, a handsome Baroque palace with gardens, a few extraordinary old houses in or near the Hauptmarkt, but apart from these the things worth seeing are essentially Roman. They lie along a firm north-south axis beginning with the Porta Nigra and ending with the towering brick building called the Basilica, a ten-minute walk away, which was built about A.D. 310.

Huge as it is, almost two hundred feet long and a hundred feet high, the Basilica was only an appendage of the imperial palace, and is thought to have been the throne room. Within, it seems to grow in size, immense because unadorned. There are no columns, no supports, nothing but the dignity of complete emptiness for its entire length and soaring to a wood ceiling. The mosaics and marble that once decorated the interior are gone, as well as the facing of the brick outside.

Though it has been robbed of its materials, been part of other buildings and put to various uses, the building—now partly restored and simplified—retains a strange grandeur.

I had not seen the Basilica before, nor do I remember the ruins of the Roman baths reached after a stroll through formal gardens. They date from the same period, part of the enormous building program that was undertaken in the waning days of the empire. Monumental and somber, the portions that remain are like molars in a vanished skull.

*

Above all this on a hillside stands the amphitheater. Then as now it is just beyond the last, neat houses at the edge of town. Past it the vineyards begin. Of the seventeen known Roman amphitheaters it is said to be the tenth largest and seated between twenty and thirty thousand people. The entrances are still impressive with their sheer retaining walls and vaulted passages, but the seats are gone. In their place are grassy slopes. It was wonderful walking along the upper rim in the soft rain. The impression is not of a great stone stadium like Rome's or Nimes's but of a large, mysterious park, a kind of burial mound. After Rome fell, the amphitheater was stripped and used as quarry. Like so many other grand designs—the necropolis at Arles, the colonnades of Leptis Magna and Sabratha—it was scattered by the winds of history and settled in untraceable fragments in castle foundations, private houses, gardens, schools.

Above are the vineyards. Walking up through them you begin to find the real Trier, the thing that has endured. The soil is steep and slate strewn. The vines are in rows as true as surveyor's lines. There are distant views of the city, misty and brown. You can hear the voices of people tending the grapes, family groups in raincoats, almost hidden by the vines. Moselle wines are, of course, world famous. Light, with low alcoholic content and a delicate acrid taste, they are best drunk when young. The best Moselles begin around Trier and continue for forty or fifty miles towards Coblenz, along the banks on both sides, vineyard after vineyard, endless, like fields of corn.

Architecture and food. Not far from the Hauptmarkt, walled and with its own cloister, is Fassbender's Central Hotel, the main part of which was built in 1268 as a private house, which then became a Benedictine abbey. The owner and chef, Charlie Fassbender, has more or less kept it the way it was. A huge, pink man with a deep voice and bushy, arched eyebrows, he can usually be found in his kitchen, which is across the main corridor from the dining room and visible through the service opening. Fassbender, who inherited the hotel from his father, is head of the Trier hotel owners' association, a local favorite and an encouraging sight to those who have come to the restaurant for the first time.

The dining room of the Central, large and high ceilinged, draws a local clientele, solid and well-dressed but not stuffy. The food is excellent and the prices reasonable. Fassbender started out as a ship's cook on the Italia, which travelled from Hamburg to New York and down to the West Indies, and the experience has given him a kind of insouciance as well as adding to his legend. A lot of English visitors come to the hotel. "They like the atmosphere of these older houses," he says. They also used to come to the old Porta Nigra Hotel, where he did his earliest apprenticeship.

Very little goes on in Trier during the winter. The bad weather comes, the ice and cold, the tourists disappear and the town turns in on itself. The dining room of the Central remains one of the beacons. Asked if he knew many of the people who were eating there that evening, Fassbender looked around for a moment. "Yes, I know them. I have time enough to learn them," he said.

I spent the last morning in the Landesmuseum, the archeological museum, which has a grim exterior but within is handsome. In its collections are many impressive pieces, parts of buildings, facades, statues, altars, as well as scale models of the major structures of the city as they once existed. It is the massiveness that impresses, the ambition with which Rome was quarried. We possess only the smallest, broken measure of what it once was, but that measure fills one with awe. We think of Rome as an empire in a way that we do not use for any other nation. The others seem pretenders. Rome stands alone. Throughout Europe, North Africa, and the Near East its wreckage still draws the traveler and speaks a message that is haunting: this was imperial, this was lasting, this is gone.

From Trier you can take boat trips down the river as far as Coblenz, or the train and travel along the Rhine to Basel. Castles on islands in the middle of the river, castles on hilltops, vineyards, beautiful towns. It is all part of childhood pictures and fairy tales, the Europe that once was and that remains.

Walking the Downs

W alking, they say, is good for you. I had an image of myself in a tweed jacket and an old hat, a lone, contented figure strolling across the English countryside, possibly with a dog. There was no dog, and in late March, weather in England was not at its finest, but I decided to go anyway. I didn't want to backpack or sleep in a tent. Nothing so ardent. What I had in mind was vague and elegant, closer to what Chesterton found in *The Pickwick Papers* when he described a feeling of "everlasting youth—a sense as of the gods gone wandering in England."

I went to see the man at the British Tourist Authority. The offices were hard to find. They were behind a Marks & Spencer in a tall building—he couldn't describe it, he said on the telephone: "I don't even know how I find it myself."

English English, he turned out to be, in a pinching grey suit with pointed lapels, a loosely tied tie, and a silver monocle. His pet Pekingese was tethered to a chair. Ah, yes, walking. Walking was something the previous generations did, he explained.

"It's a thing of the '20s and '30s when they, um, walked

across fields. Virginia Woolf, Malcom Muggeridge, they all walked, but now, of course, with the markers, the maps, and so forth, they wouldn't do it now."

He liked to walk himself. He'd walked last year in the Cotswolds, in fact, all the villages and towns—"ruined by people like us," he added. Now you found big car parks, souvenir shops, everything real was gone. There was one fortunate thing, however. When you walk, you come back into town the back way, and then you see it as it was.

The first thing I felt I needed was some literature. At the Ramblers' Association, which is the national organization for those who enjoy walking in the countryside, there was a bewildering number of pamphlets and mimeographed sheets. At Stanford's, a shop near Covent Garden that specializes in such things, I bought three or four solid guidebooks plus some Ordnance Survey Landranger maps, without which, all authorities warned, setting forth would be folly. As usually happens I also bought a few books that I thought I might read but that would probably turn up years later with the sales slip still in them, books like Belloc's *The Path to Rome*, books on the location of famous graves in England, and so forth.

I had decided that, rather than struggle with local paths and byways, I'd try a section of one of the long-distance routes. There are thirteen of these in England and Wales, the most famous being the Pennine, about 250 miles long and passing through some of the most remote areas of upland Britain. It was described as challenging. I felt drawn to something I might be more likely to enjoy and finally settled on the South Downs Way, a mere eighty miles across rolling Sussex with views of the sea. An ancient track probably thousands of years old, it begins in Eastbourne, a handsome seaside resort almost due south of London, passes north of Brighton, continues west past Chichester to end near Petersfield. I thought I might do about half of it. I had reassuring memories of having completed infantry training, longer ago than I would like to say, with the traditional thirty-mile hike, carrying a sixty-pound pack.

There was not much equipment required. I bought a backpack, a water bottle, and a pair of lightweight Italian hiking boots that I was assured were state of the art. I wore the boots around London for a few days to break them in. I was concerned about how waterproof they were since it had been raining off and on for the two weeks I'd been in England, but they stayed perfectly dry inside. I packed a waterproof parka, a corduroy hat, a pair of khaki trousers, shirts, and a sweater. Lastly, I put in toilet articles, a jackknife, a one-day-old *Paris Trib*, and a couple of oranges. Early the next morning I caught the train to Eastbourne from Victoria Station. There was the shrill whistle of the conductor, the slamming of coach doors; goodbye to all that.

*

London was grey in mist. We crossed the Thames, past power plants, drab industrial areas, endless suburbs one would never visit. Ten thousand chimneys, countless rows of houses, and then suddenly playing fields, emerald in the midst. Lines of Betjeman drifted through my head, *Dear old, bloody old England, / Of telephone poles and tin* ... Past Gatwick the countryside began: lines of trees, green fields, home of the badger and fox. Finally there were broad, open coastal lands—the sea.

Walking down to the beach from the station in Eastbourne, I paused to buy the *Ward Lock Red Guide to Sussex*. I was already carrying a guidebook called *South Downs Way*, a pocket edition of *The Compleat Angler*, and various maps and pamphlets including one called *Out in the Country*, published by the Countryside Commission, outlining what might be called the rules of the game. It was a punishable offense, for instance, to keep a bull in a field crossed by a right-of-way, but there were certain exceptions: bulls less than eleven months old, bulls not belonging to one of the recognized dairy breeds, in each case as long as accompanied by heifers or cows. . . . I pondered this as I walked. (I weighed a copy of the *Ward Lock Red Guide* not long ago. It was three quarters of a pound—not much, but a major infraction of a primary rule, which is never carry an ounce you do not have to.)

A cold rain began to fall as I walked down the wide seafront of Eastbourne. Soon I was on a promenade above the sea, sheltered by majestic cedars or pines, the stony beach far below. Ahead was a kiosk mentioned in the guide and the grassy hillside that was the start of the path. I felt a slight uneasiness as if just before a military operation—would I find the route, would I get someplace by dark? I climbed the hill. There were rooks in the great empty meadows where silent country rolled down to the sea, timeless country, unimproved, unspoiled. The grass was soft underfoot and very short, kept that way by grazing sheep, though the ones I saw were far inland.

Eastbourne and its streets and houses—in one of them

Darwin wrote portions of the *Origin of Species*—were visible behind. To the left, the steep chalk cliffs that cut down to the Channel grew higher. It became the edge of the world, unfenced and unguarded. It was hundreds of feet straight down to the surf that was shattering itself against the chalk. A few miles farther was the highest point, Beachy Head, with its famous solitary lighthouse more than five hundred feet below. It's possible to descend here by a steep path to another lighthouse, now a private residence, Belle Tout, two miles further west, and from there go along the sea to Birling Gap, a natural cut in the cliffs, but I was reluctant to give up the heights.

At Birling Gap is a small hotel and pub. I had lunch and warmed myself at the electric fireplace. "Where did you walk from?" they inquired.

"Eastbourne."

"Are you going back?"

"No, I'm going on to Alfriston."

It was a little past noon.

"Are you a fast walker?" they asked.

Past Birling Gap are the Seven Sisters, magnificent chalk cliffs rising and falling for about two miles and ending at a valley where a small river called Cuckmere flows to the sea. From there the way goes inland to West Dean and farther, to Alfriston. Now begins an England you would not otherwise see: walls, walkways, great flint houses with their brick coigns, village churches with wood-timbered roofs and records of priests' names going back unbroken for nearly a thousand years. In every church are the carved stones and bronze plaques in memory of sons and husbands who were killed in 1915, 1916, 1918, and names of insignificant towns in France where thousands fell. Time stopped for England then and for unmarried girls, sisters, parents. In the once-famous curtain lines of Noël Coward's *Cavalcade*, the lady of the house holds up her glass on New Year's Eve years after the war and drinks to her sons and "to our hearts that died with them."

In the rain I lingered by churches and alongside fences through which could be seen silent estates. There were extraordinary houses that seemed to have been there for gen-erations, even centuries, houses built to a standard different from our own. Even the gardens with their stone dovecotes and sloping lawns, a glimpse of which could be had through wrought-iron arches or gates, were there for the ages.

In the dusk I crossed a footbridge into Alfriston. There were a number of cars parked on the far side, among them a pearl-grey Rolls. I took the Rolls to be a mark of civilization and certain standards of accommodation, and it turned out I was right. Alfriston had a wealth of good places to spend the night. I ended up in one called The Old Apiary on the main street. Among its comforts was listed "constant hot water." I had a good room with a large bed and windows overlooking the river. A long hot bath, half a bottle of wine and a chicken pie at the pub just down the road seemed as great a luxury as I can remember, and I fell into bed with the rain pouring down.

*

With morning came clear skies and the sound of birds. A large English breakfast waited in the dining room. I was one of two overnight guests though I never saw the other. There were only two rooms, and there is, they say, a good chance of getting one without a reservation except on weekends during July and August.

The Apiary is I-don't-know-how-many centuries old. When the roof was repaired a few years ago, the roofers, making the best match they could, used tiles 250 years old. Down the street is an older place called the Star Inn, which dates from the fifteenth century and has outside a carved figurehead of a lion salvaged from a seventeenth-century shipwreck. It had modernized rooms and a large dining room, and had I seen it first I might have stayed there, although it would have cost the equivalent of four nights at The Apiary—the bill there having been £14 (about $25). Close to the river in Alfriston is St. Andrew's, called the Cathedral of the South Downs, dating from the fourteenth century and a notable example of flint work. Near it is the thatched-roof Clergy House. Equally ancient, it has the distinction of being the first property to be acquired by the National Trust. That was in 1896. The price was £10.

I walked several miles to Berwick to see a small church with once-scandalous murals by Quentin and Vanessa Bell, but the church was locked. A note advised knocking on the vestry door for the key, but no one was at the vestry. The sun was climbing and the road beckoned.

The way led across great rolling hills. I saw many hoofprints but never a horse or rider, not another soul in fact, until about noon when three walkers, husband, wife, and grown son came along. I had been right about imagining myself with a dog. They had a beautiful corgi, white-chested, blazing in the sun, trotting beside them. Later I saw a solitary girl, also with a dog, up ahead, walking the empty downs. After awhile she disappeared. From the tops of the hills the sea was visible—the Channel, turquoise with a long bank of fair weather clouds above it. I had fresh rolls and some fruit in my knapsack, and I more or less ate as I walked. I didn't want to stop. I wanted to bathe in the long, luxurious miles.

There were occasional tumuli—ancient burial mounds. The South Downs has nearly a thousand of these great round barrows in which Bronze Age peoples buried their dead. Once nearly fifteen or twenty feet high, they have been worn down by time, and all have been plundered, typically through the top so that they now have a central depression in them.

You begin to feel you are heir to all this—the stretches of forest, the irregular villages below, the quiet roofs. The aristocracy rides—it is part of the image, a Jaguar and fine clothes, a glimpse of a beautiful face in the blue of the windshield—but everybody rides nowadays. The true luxury is away from all that, on lands that may be crossed but are not to be bought, in silence except for the wind, in timelessness except for the lowering sun.

*

Sometime in mid-afternoon I reached the Ouse River near Rodmell, and Monk's House, in which Virginia Woolf lived from 1919 until her death in 1941. The house, right on the lane, is clapboard in front with greenhouses and long gardens in back and a sign advising that it is open on Wednesdays and Saturdays between 2:00 and 6:00 PM. The day happened to be a Thursday—it's a good idea to carry, or better, consult a book like *Historic Houses, Castles, and Gardens in Great Britain and Ireland*, which can be found in almost any bookshop, to determine when places can be visited. Only churches, as a rule, are reliably open. Unable to enter Monk's House, I thought I would walk down to the river, presumably along the very path that Woolf, depressed and fearful that madness was claiming her, walked on the way to drowning herself. I had always pictured Monk's House as practically on the banks of the river and the fated walk down a sort of lawn. In fact the river is far off, a thirty-minute walk, along a dirt track through pastures. It's a muddy river, more like a canal, the banks man-made, high, and bare. Looking back across the low farmland, I could barely see the house. In the choppy brown water, moving slowly upstream, a single white swan appeared, feeding along the bank.

Keeping to the embankment I walked to Lewes, the handsome, ancient marketing city where in centuries past the Ouse, once a broad estuary, narrowed. In a French restaurant on High Street where they were setting the tables for dinner, I asked if there was a decent place nearby to stay. I ended up on a downhill, curving street called Rotten Row, about five minutes away, at a bed-and-breakfast called Hillside. The house belonged to two sisters, one a retired schoolteacher and the other a caterer named Hollins. It had been their parents' house, and they had only recently dedicated it, or at least several rooms in it, to tourism. From these ladies, I learned among other things that Rotten Row was probably a mispronunciation of Route du Roi—the road along which the

French king came into Lewes—from the days of the Norman invasion. This part of England was overrun for three hundred years, and William the Conqueror parceled out Sussex to his favorite companions. There are many French names here, and there's a French look to many buildings and lanes.

One can easily spend a day in Lewes, which, it turned out, is what I did since in the morning it was raining again and my knees were giving notice that the memorable thirty-mile infantry hike had been a long time ago. Having read a superb small guidebook called *Historic Lewes*, I visited the ruins of the castle that looks out over the town, the church with its tomb of one of the Conqueror's daughters, a jewel of a museum in a sixteenth-century timber-framed house that had belonged to Anne of Cleves, and an exceptional hotel called Shelleys, Georgian in style and patrician in feeling, where Samuel Johnson once stayed and where I will probably stay next time. I ducked out of the rain and had lunch at the King's Head, a pub near the church.

*

The trains between Lewes and London run hourly; late in the day I took one (a trip of about an hour) and that night had dinner with friends from the States. We ate at The Connaught, which, apart from serving some of the best food in London, is about as far from a bed-and-breakfast as it is possible to get on one sceptered island. Before going to The Connaught and while soaking my legs in a hot bath, I looked at a map to see how far I had walked. It was about three inches.

I had meant to go farther, having as a vague objective a

house called Uppark, which is near the western end of the
South Downs Way. It was built about 1690 and later was the
scene of debauchery and riotous parties, at one of which a
young girl named Emma Hart, who had been brought down
from London as a plaything, danced naked, it is said, on the
table and was admired greatly by one of the guests, an older
man, Sir William Hamilton, who eventually obtained her by
paying off her protector's debts. She lived with him in Naples
where he was the British ambassador. A few years later he
married her and she became Lady Hamilton. She met an English admiral, Horatio Nelson, and from this point on the
story is well-known.

Uppark and its eighteenth-century furnishings and pictures are intact. It was offered to the Duke of Wellington by
his grateful government, but when he saw the hill going up
to the place, he is said to have decided against it and commented that he would have been put to the expense of new
horses every year and a half if he accepted.

*

I took one other walk about a week later, up the Thames
from London to Windsor and then on to Maidenhead. It
lasted three days. I thought it would be both pastoral and
historic, a leisurely journey beside England's great river.
Along the way there is Hampton Court, a cardinal's great
palace that Henry VIII coolly appropriated and then, even
more haughtily, added on to. Windsor is equally interesting,
but for the most part the journey itself is disappointing. It
passes through what was once called Metroland, the careless

bedroom suburbs where the pleasures of country life vanish in drab houses and dispirited towns. The river is cluttered with cheap dwellings and noisy boats, and the walk might be compared to walking from JFK to Manhattan. If you ask for directions in pubs, the bartenders invariably apologize that they are not from this part of the country. There is hardly a minute that an airliner coming or going from Heathrow is not passing overhead.

Beyond Windsor, pleasant enough if you stay in one of the good hotels and eat in a restaurant by the river, there is some improvement. The ugly bungalows and cottages disappear. There are open fields and mudcaked ponies hanging their necks over the fences. Along the path are hedges, willows, grass tennis courts, and approaching Maidenhead, the thrilling sight of the brick railway bridge with its two long, low arches, built by Brunel in 1839 and immortalized in Turner's bold, impressionistic *Rain, Steam, and Speed*. The painting is in the National Gallery, and the bridge still in use, as graceful and smoothly mortared as it was a hundred fifty years ago. It's a great thing to hear the cold, incoming rush and see a sleek blue Intercity streak across the perfectly engineered span.

If I were to attempt the Thames again I would do Kew Gardens and Richmond from London itself, then next day take the train to Hampton Court and afterwards to Windsor. The walk should begin from there.

Details of Lady Hamilton's early years are not plentiful. She was nearly illiterate and probably had a child when she was sixteen. She was the mistress first of a naval officer, then a doctor, and then began sleeping with the well-born. Along the way she picked up some slight education and learned to sing, dance, and act. She was beautiful and her personality vivid. Naples, with its prodigious immorality, taught her extravagance, and after a largely glorious life she died in poverty. I picture Uppark, the scene of one of the great turning points in the drama, as beautifully situated, elegant, and pale. There is the gleam of old wood, the fine lines of crafted furniture, and large windows with views that position and wealth afford. The scale of the rooms fills one with a sense of well-being and vague images of life as it ought to be lived. I know there is quite a hill to be climbed beforehand and also the distinct possibility that the grounds will be closed that day, but sometime I hope to walk there.

Paumanok

I woke in a Los Angeles bedroom. It was dark, the curtains drawn. A voice I did not recognize was speaking, a strange voice and words I heard in a daze. Somehow I could not find my place in them. There was a small red light. From the corner of my eye I made it out to be the clock radio, the numbers trembling. It was a few minutes past nine, and I was floating in the wake of dreams. In deep tones a voice was speaking,

Once Paumanok, when the lilac-scent was in the air and Fifth-month grass was growing . . .

What is this, I thought? I know this.

Two feather'd guests from Alabama, two together . . . And every day the he-bird to and fro . . . And every day the she-bird crouch'd on her nest, silent, with bright eyes, and every day I, a curious boy, never too close, never disturbing them . . .

Slowly the awnings and perfect lawns fell away, the office buildings, palms, and streets, and I was filled with longing. The great lyric of Whitman's, the song of my youth, filled the darkness of the house like a manifesto,

*...all summer in the sound of the sea, and at night under the full moon
...over the hoarse surging sea, or flitting from brier to brier by day, I saw,
I heard at intervals the remaining one...*

I lay there, the blood draining from my face. Paumanok—
the long, bare beaches of the east, the fields, the weathered
houses, I saw them again, I felt them calling. Across the
desert, the cattlelands, the rivers, the cities in the Midwest. I
closed my eyes. It was the thirty-first of May, Walt Whitman's birthday, and I lay beside him as a soldier might lie by
his captain, heartsick, dreaming of home.

Paumanok is the Indian name of Long Island, the eastern
end of which has always seemed like England to me, insular,
green, with treacherous weather and not quite modern life.
Its farms and houses are old and well-established; they create
the landscape rather than being situated in it. Like England
there are strong literary ties, writers and editors in great numbers. Bridgehampton with its single street is their London.
There are houses here in which I have written parts of books,
met publishers, and where from windows in the morning
looked out on empty fields in which geese stood.

Days by the sea, something one never forgets. The dunes,
the green Atlantic, with only a few cars in the morning
parked along the sandy road. Far down, in the haze, in front
of a large house a flag waves, the red, white, and blue pure as
the sky. It seems like the '20s, the vanished emptiness of the
south of France; the flag in the distance might be flying over
the Murphy's Villa America. Time has disappeared; the sun
bears down. From time to time a small plane flies by.

There is no taste like the taste of the sea. In solid ranks,
the waves come in. The water is heavy; it tumbles down like

cement. Every so often there is a chilling moment when the
sea withdraws leaving only a foot or two of water in front of a
huge wave about to break. The day is at its zenith. In a chair
facing the horizon a girl with her hair tied back, slim-limbed,
sits reading a book. Later she lies back, glistening with oil,
beneath the sun.

People come here for the usual reasons, to sail, play tennis, meet other people. The summer holds the promise of
love affairs, novels written, barefoot life. The summer seems
to simplify, to enable. In the evenings, skin still feverish from
the sun, you dine on flounder, potatoes, cold white wine. The
food belongs to paradise. It seems to come from a world that
no longer exists, the world of the Impressionists, rich har-
vests and serene days. At the roadside stands goats wearing
sun visors lie drowsily beneath the trees, and corn picked
that morning is heaped on wooden tables.

August dinners. The moussaka is finished, the two bottles
of Echézaux. They are telling stories of the wrecks long ago,
the wreck of the *Louis Philippe*, the wreck of the *Circassian*
when a salvage crew of forty Indians was put aboard while
the storm was still raging and the ship slowly capsized. The
Indians had climbed into the rigging but they all drowned.
"An inauspicious circassian," a Brahmin comments. Dinner at
Bobby Van's. The great, throaty laugh of Gloria Jones, her
passionate cry, *"Jamais de ma vie!"* Dinners on Sagg Road,
swimming afterwards in the thunderous sea, dark and windy,
not a light anywhere, shouting to be heard and stumbling
from the surf searching for clothes.

*

And so it ends. The long lines of weekend traffic leave. In the grass by the roadside a dog trots anxiously looking for the people who have abandoned him. Last picnics on the beach in the evening, ears of corn soaked in seawater and roasted over embers, the final piece of bread dropped butter-side down in the sand. The old houses seem empty. The first leaves blow along the road. In the evening the geese come over in long, uneven V's, their necks extended.

The end of the season has come, perhaps the best time of all, silence and perfect days. One final hour by the sea. On the almost empty sand, a crab claw, two young boys and their mother, a cigar band, a half-naked girl. *Ave.*

James Salter's books include five novels, *The Hunters, Cassada, A Sport and a Pastime, Light Years, Solo Faces,* and two memoirs, *Burning the Days* and *Gods of Tin.* His second collection of short stories, *Last Night,* was recently published, and followed *Dusk and Other Stories,* which was awarded the PEN/Faulkner Prize in 1989. Commissioned as a regular officer in the Air Force in 1945, he was a fighter pilot and flew more than a hundred missions during the Korean War. He resigned his commission in 1957 in order to devote himself to writing. A member of the American Academy and Institute of Arts and Letters, he divides his time between New York and Colorado.